TRANSFORMATIONAL TEACHING

TRANSFORMATIONAL TEACHING

WALDORF-INSPIRED METHODS IN THE PUBLIC SCHOOL

MARY GORAL

SteinerBooks

STEINERBOOKS
An imprint of Anthroposophic Press, Inc.
402 Union Street, No. 58
Hudson, NY 12534
www.steinerbooks.org

Design: William Jens Jensen
Cover photo © by First Class Photos PTY Ltd.

Library of Congress Cataloging-in-Publication Data

Goral, Mary.

Transformational teaching : Waldorf-inspired methods in the
public schools / Mary Goral.

p. cm.

Includes bibliographical references.

ISBN 978-0-88010-704-4

1. Waldorf method of education—United States. 2. Public
schools—United States. I. Title.

LB1029.W34G67 2009

371.39'1—dc22

2009002299

CONTENTS

INTRODUCTION   vii

1. WALDORF EDUCATION   1

2. THE WALDORF-INSPIRED CADRE   15

3. BUILDING COMMUNITY   46

4. ENGAGING STUDENTS   66

5. THE INNER LIFE OF THE TEACHER   89

6. LOOKING TOWARD THE FUTURE WITH HOPE   112

    APPENDICES   141

    BIBLIOGRAPHY   153

DEDICATION

For the teachers in the Waldorf-inspired Cadre. May they always believe in themselves and in their understanding of how best to educate their students.

GRATITUDE

First and foremost, I would like to thank the members of the Waldorf-inspired Cadre, specifically those teachers who allowed me to come into their classrooms and who spent time talking with me about their educational beliefs and philosophies: Brenda Chelliah, Kelly Cole, Barbara Doyle, Jennifer Geroski, Patty Gilderbloom, Jenny Heath, Mona Jones, Jan Kovac, Debbie Lockyear, Tina Marsteller, Brad Nance, Jo Anne Noland, Shawna Stenton, Donna Stottman, Laura Wasz, Kathy Learn, and Patty Rundell. I also thank principals Shannon Conlon and Kris Raitzer.

Without the pioneering work of Caroline Pinné, this book and the Cadre project would not have been possible. Her dedication and perseverance to Waldorf-inspired practices in the public-school setting has resulted in thousands of children receiving the education they deserve.

Special gratitude goes to Janey Newton and the Norton Foundation. Her vision and generosity is unparalleled.

Many thanks go to the people at SteinerBooks, including Gene Gollogly, who believed the message in this book was meant to be heard; Evander Lompke, for reading and rereading the manuscript; and Steve Sagarin, for his insightful critique.

Thanks also go to Janiece Jaffe and Julie Hennessey, who opened their homes and hearts to me throughout the writing of this book.

Finally, my ultimate gratitude goes to my husband Bill and my children, Sam, Tom, Zach, Samantha, and Tony. Their love and support have allowed this book to reach fruition.

INTRODUCTION

"WHAT IS WALDORF?" I asked our tour guide who was leading my colleague and I through Findhorn, a small cooperative community located on Scotland's North Sea. "Get a book in the bookstore and read about it," he replied. Apparently, the rest of the people on the tour did not require a detailed answer to my question about where the children at Findhorn go to school.

Although I had studied and worked in the field of education for nearly twenty years, I had never heard of Waldorf education. As is typical for many educators in the United States, this deeply innovative and creative approach to schooling had escaped me through my entire career, which includes an undergraduate degree in elementary education, a master's in mathematics education, eleven years of teaching in the public schools, and the coursework for my doctorate in curriculum studies. I had to travel 3,000 miles across the Atlantic Ocean to discover what would become my life's work. Fortunately, Francis Edmund's *Rudolf Steiner Education: The Waldorf School* (1992), a classic book on the subject, opened a whole new world for me.

After returning to the U.S., I immediately located the Waldorf school closest to my university and arranged a visit. Although five hours away, it was well worth the trip. As soon as I walked through the doors of the school, I knew I had come home. This was the type of school I had been searching for my entire life. I made preliminary arrangements to begin a year-long qualitative study on Waldorf education.

The following September, I arrived at the Rudolf Steiner School in Ann Arbor, Michigan. After a few short weeks, I knew my initial idea of focusing on how mathematics is taught in a Waldorf school was ultimately too narrow. Owing to the holistic nature of Waldorf education, I could not limit my study to one subject area. After another month of study, I knew that I had to focus my work on how this amazing approach to education could be applied in the public-school setting. All children deserved to be taught this way.

Seventeen years have passed since my initial discovery, and my innate knowing that Waldorf education desperately needed to make its way into the lives of public-school children. During this decade and a half, a number of Waldorf-inspired initiatives have sprung up across North America. Currently, there are a number of public Waldorf methods charter schools, including; eighteen in California, five in Arizona, four in Oregon, two in Alaska, one in Colorado, one in Texas, one in Hawaii, and three in Quebec. Two additional charter school initiatives are in the works in California. Other public initiatives include the Urban Waldorf School in Milwaukee, Wisconsin, and the Waldorf-inspired Cadre—a group of public-school teachers in Louisville, Kentucky, who use Waldorf-inspired methods in their classrooms.

This book focuses on the small group of teachers—The Waldorf-inspired Cadre in Louisville—who are making a tremendous difference in the lives of their students, and who have been deeply changed by their experiences with Waldorf education. In addition, I will outline the unique attributes of the Waldorf-inspired Cadre Project. Before discussing the Cadre and their work with public-school children, I will offer a brief overview of Waldorf education, followed by a history of the Cadre. The following chapters focus on the positive impact that Waldorf-inspired methods have on public-school children and offer ways that public-school teachers can integrate this engaging pedagogy into their own classrooms.

WALDORF EDUCATION

W E HAVE THE POWER to transform our public schools—not through the latest and greatest educational research, definitely not through government mandates or the newest "teacher proof" text series, or even through what many educators call "best practices." I firmly believe that our schools can be transformed by applying Waldorf-inspired practices into the public-school setting. This little-known, but well-established form of education can be a source of ideas and strategies to teachers, administrators, and teacher educators. In a 1994 interview, Elliott Eisner noted:

> Waldorf education possesses unique educational features that have considerable potential for improving public education in America. The time is ripe for public schools to explore the ways in which ideas in Waldorf education might be explored in their own settings. For too long, in my opinion, Waldorf education has been on the margins of education. It needs to receive the kind of attention it deserves. (Urmacher 1994)

Waldorf education can no longer be one of the "best-kept" secrets in North America. Nor, as Urmacher (1991, x) stated, should Waldorf schools be "marching quietly along, unheard." Furthermore, it is past time that those involved in the Waldorf movement step to the fore-front and begin educating the public. In the words of Betty Staley

(1997), director of the high-school teacher training at Rudolf Steiner College in California, "The Waldorf movement is challenged to educate the public about the essentials of Waldorf education, to speak out for the soul needs of children, and to call attention to the damaging effects that our society is having on children's lives" (p. 30).

Although educators have called for Waldorf-inspired education to be a viable part of public schools for over fifteen years, only a few forward-thinking programs around the country have implemented some form of Waldorf education into their public schools. As previously mentioned in the introduction, one such program is alive and well in Louisville, Kentucky. The Jefferson County Public Schools have a number of teachers who are members of the Waldorf-inspired Cadre—a group of innovative public educators who integrate Waldorf-inspired methods into their classrooms. Before delving into their story, however, it is helpful to offer a brief history and background of Waldorf education. By looking at the roots and history of Waldorf education as well as the philosophy, curriculum, and pedagogy found in Waldorf schools, I hope to inform the Waldorf novice and offer a foundation for those interested in bringing Waldorf-inspired teaching to the public-school setting. If, however, the reader already possesses a strong background in all things Waldorf, skip this chapter and move on to chapter two.

THE ROOTS OF WALDORF EDUCATION

Because Waldorf education continues to be one of the best-kept secrets in this country, few know about Waldorf schools and their origin.

Waldorf schools are the second largest nondenominational group of alternative schools in the world, with over 2,000 schools, including between 200 and 300 (closer to 300 if we include charter schools that use methods inspired by Waldorf education) in the United States. Created by Dr. Rudolf Steiner shortly after World War I, the first Waldorf school was intended for the children of the workers of the Waldorf-Astoria Cigarette Factory in Stuttgart, Germany. Emil Molt, the president of the factory, asked Steiner to create the school because he had studied Steiner's philosophical works. He felt that an educational approach incorporating Steiner's theories of the developing human being would be a practical way to implement Steiner's threefold social ideas and counteract the prevailing mechanistic worldview in Germany. Steiner, a controversial figure in the cultural life of Central Europe and a prolific writer and lecturer on philosophy, medicine, religion, and education, designed the school to meet the ever-changing educational and spiritual needs of children in an industrial society.

Steiner saw Molt's invitation as an opportunity to develop an educational method not only to meet the intellectual needs of children, but also to meet their spiritual needs. Steiner held that education must meet the needs of the whole child—body, spirit, and soul, or "head, hands, and heart" (Koetzsch 1989).

To understand how Steiner intended to meet the needs of the whole child, it is important to take a brief look at his theory of child development. According to Steiner (1995), body, spirit, and soul are profoundly interrelated, and a child develops toward adulthood in roughly seven-year stages, through which the body, soul, and spirit come into tandem with one another (Edmunds 1992; Reinsmith 1989). With each stage, specific spiritual and psychological changes occur simultaneously with physical changes.

From birth to about age seven, children exist entirely in their senses (Steiner 1995). After leaving the womb, a child is exposed to new environments and soaks up each situation like a sponge. Learning permeates a child's entire being through active imitation. Children grow not only outwardly, but also inwardly, forming their individual instrument according to each child's human potential (Edmunds 1992; Urmacher 1991).

The second seven-year stage begins approximately with the loss of the baby teeth. Whereas children learn primarily through imitation during the first stage, they apprehend mainly through feeling and imagination during the second stage. According to Steiner (1995), the child now experiences the world as an artist and learns about the world through story, parable, and myth. Teachers must translate the intellectual content of the curriculum into age-appropriate methods in order to arouse the feelings that form the basis of the mind's later development (Barnes 1980; Reinsmith 1989; Urmacher 1991).

The third stage of development begins with adolescence. It is characterized by a new level of consciousness: the intellect. Children are now ready to conceptualize the laws that underlie phenomena. Educators must push children to judge, critique, and examine more abstractly and to become more aware of the world. Around the age of twenty-one, the "I" begins to awaken (Steiner 1995), at which point the individual begins to accept moral accountability and to become a responsible, contributing member of society (Barnes 1980; Koetzsch 1989; Reinsmith 1989; Urmacher 1991).

The explicit purpose of Waldorf schools has always been to develop free, independent, moral, and creative human beings. Steiner proposed that this could be accomplished in several ways: teaching a developmentally appropriate curriculum rooted in the humanities; having the teacher remain with the same group of children for at least a few years during elementary school; and valuing equally the arts and crafts and the traditional academic subjects. Because Steiner saw each human being as spiritual and having a divine spark, one purpose of Waldorf education is to protect and feed that inner quality and educate the heart, soul, and mind of each child.

Because Steiner's worldview and orientation toward education was based on his spiritual views, it is rare to find his educational philosophy included in traditional textbooks for teacher training. This is one reason why educators in North America are generally unfamiliar with Waldorf methods. It is nevertheless interesting that many of the ideas undergirding Steiner's educational philosophy can be traced to the theories of several well-known educational philosophers, including Rousseau, Froebel, and Pestalozzi.

As mentioned, Steiner thought that education should be grounded in an understanding of child development, which begins with imitation, proceeds through imagination, and culminates in the intellect. Like Steiner, Jean-Jacques Rousseau (1712–1778) believed that education should promote and encourage qualities such as cheerfulness, spontaneity, and the inquisitiveness associated with childhood. Rousseau also held that education should be developmentally appropriate and that young children should not be instructed in academic subjects at an early age.

Following Rousseau, was Johann Pestalozzi (1746–1827), a Swiss educator who agreed with and built upon Rousseau's ideas. Both Steiner and Pestalozzi believed that education is based on sensory impressions and that children would reach their natural potential through proper sensory impressions. Pestalozzi referred to this as "object lessons," which provide children with manipulative experiences that lead naturally to particular concepts. It is interesting that Steiner spoke directly against Pestalozzi's object lessons, noting that sensory impressions are only one pole of experience and that, therefore, education includes reaching children through all of their intelligences. Both theorists believed, however, that the best teachers are those who teach *children,* not subjects.

According to Gutek, in his informative text *Pestalozzi and Education* (1968), Pestalozzi felt that schools should focus on the harmonious development of the human, the "development of all his human powers and capacities" (p. 30), and that such development should occur in a climate of emotional security. Like Steiner, Pestalozzi believed in a balanced education of head, heart, and hands. Pestalozzi was critical of traditional education that separated thinking and doing (Gutek 1968).

Friedrich Froebel (1782–1852), another holistic educator who actually attended one of Pestalozzi's institutes believed that, through education, the human being's divine essence is brought forth (Froebel 1887). According to Froebel, teachers should learn with the children and learning should be adapted to the children's needs. He saw nature as a prime source for learning and felt that manual work was ennobling.

Froebel's concept of children and how they learn was based, in part, on the idea of *unfolding,* a concept also held by Pestalozzi and Steiner. The educator's role was to observe this natural unfolding of children and provide activities enabling them to learn when they are ready to learn. In addition to school subjects, Froebel, like Steiner, held that children should work in the field and garden, experience woodworking and weaving, model with clay, and paint. Like Pestalozzi and Steiner, Froebel believed that school was to be an extension of the home with both work and play activities. He believed in establishing an emotionally secure environment and in the importance of early childhood education with a focus on play rather than academics. In Froebel's (1887) words, "Play is the highest phase of child development of this period" (p. 54). Steiner (1996) also stressed the importance of play in the early childhood setting.

> To a healthy child, playing is in no way just a pleasurable pastime, but a completely serious activity. Play flows earnestly from a child's entire organism. If your way of teaching can capture the child's seriousness in play, you will not merely teach in a playful way—in the ordinary sense—but you will nurture the earnestness of a child's play. (pp. 61–62)

Consistent with the idea of unfolding, Froebel believed that young children are like flowers blooming from a bud and that with love and care, children will grow and someday produce fruit. Froebel likened the role of educator to that of a gardener, and, like Steiner, Froebel believed young children needed to be cared for and loved. Steiner repeatedly stresses the importance of educator/teacher love for students in many different lectures. In a 1922 lecture, Steiner (2004) states, "In a Waldorf school, who the teachers are is far more important than any technical ability they may have acquired intellectually. It is important that teachers not only love the children, but also love the whole procedure they use" (p. 56).

Many of the theories and philosophies of education mentioned here can be found throughout Waldorf education, from the belief in the importance of children's developmental stages to the idea that children need to be respected as spiritual beings and whose highest potential should always be kept in mind. The following section describes in detail several of the key principles from Waldorf education, principles reflective of these practices that could easily be applied to the public-school setting.

WALDORF ENVIRONMENT, CURRICULUM, AND INSTRUCTION

To help the reader gain a better understanding of Waldorf education, it is useful to explore it through three domains; the environment of the school, curriculum, and pedagogy. Several important factors contribute to an understanding of a school's environment, not the least of which are a school's philosophy/vision, the physical environment of a school, and a sense of community.

Philosophy and Vision. All schools, whether public or private, need to be grounded in a common theory or philosophy. This philosophy can be used as a lens through which one can reflect and work. A school's philosophy, also known as its *vision*, unites a school with a bond of shared understandings and common language. It involves a commitment from parents and teachers, as well as administrators, and provides an avenue where everyone can come together for reflective conversations based on a common goal.

Steiner initiated Waldorf schools to counteract a trend of the time—the move toward an increasingly mechanistic, analytical, and exclusively intellectual educational environment. He believed that spirituality was a crucial component of every child's education. This spiritual approach is not based on any one religion but refers to the spiritual nature of the human being and the divine spark in each child. Steiner held a particular interest in the education of children and saw schooling as a way to achieve social renewal (Sturbaum 1997). According to formal brochures and literature, the philosophy of the Waldorf school is oriented toward assisting the healthy development of head, hand, and heart in order to create loving, compassionate students who love learning for its own sake.

> Steiner's philosophy of education...seeks to address the full and harmonious development of the child's spiritual, emotional, and physical capacities so that he may act in life as a self-disciplined and morally responsible human being. (Association of Waldorf Schools of North America [AWSNA] 1992, 2)

What tends to make Waldorf education unique, is that this philosophy is deeply embedded within the school's environment, as well as in the curriculum and instruction.

Physical Environment. The philosophy inherent in the design of a Waldorf school contends that classrooms should not be over-stimulating, so that children can focus better. Although colors may vary from school to school, many private Waldorf schools in the U.S. paint classrooms using a technique referred to as "lazure" (with various colors for different ages: pastel pink for early childhood, pastel orange for first grade, pastel yellow for second grade). They are furnished and decorated beautifully, yet sparingly. Fresh flowers, candles, plants, and low-level lighting afford students an aesthetically pleasing environment that appeals to their senses. The importance of beauty is also reflected in the classroom "tools." Toys and "manipulatives" in the early childhood and kindergarten classrooms, for example, are made of organic and natural substances (wood, cotton gauze, and beeswax). The children in kindergarten and early childhood education are provided with materials for *constructive* creative play, rather than being given finished, manufactured, or processed toys. Rawson and Richter (2000) stress the importance of the environment in a Waldorf kindergarten classroom:

> The kindergarten staff spend hours in their kindergartens both before the children arrive in the morning and after they have gone. There are activities and materials to prepare, of course, but more importantly there has to be the right mood in place. The staff often meets in the morning to say a verse together before going to their rooms to be there when the children arrive. (pp. 33–34)

David Orr (1999) believes that, "more than any other institution in modern society, education has a moral stake in the health, beauty, and integrity of the world our students will inherit" (p. 147). Waldorf schools make a point of offering a beautiful environment for children of all ages. Moreover, the simple, soothing atmosphere of the Waldorf classroom promotes a calm sense of peace in the children. Waldorf philosophy contends that teachers must be very conscious of the physical environment and the impression it makes on children.

For those educators seriously interested in changing their school's environment, a tour of a Waldorf school is suggested. Not only does the focus on aesthetics provide a beautiful setting for children, it helps students build "sensitivity to subtle relationships, to harmony and balance that will underlie their sense of self, learning, life, and even a society to work toward" (Byers, Dillard, Easton, Manry, McDermott, Oberman, and Urmacher 1996, 40).

Community through Continuity. For years, conventional elementary schools have placed students in graded classrooms and handed them off from one teacher to the next, year after year. After fifth or sixth grade, students are sent to a completely different school, one that is highly departmentalized and possibly tracked. There is no sense of continuity for the children, which is sad because school is often the only stable place in many of today's children's lives. In order to combat this disjointed experience, many Waldorf teachers ideally stay with their classes from first through eighth grade, though Steiner recommended only that teachers stay with their classes for at least a few years. Waldorf early-childhood educators, too, remain with their kindergarten children for two or three years (Waldorf kindergarten is a two- to three-year experience). The children and the teacher establish a community within the first year (first grade) and continue to grow and learn together throughout their Waldorf schooling. Relationships between students and teacher deepen with each passing year. Class teachers are responsible for the progress and academic growth of each student, giving the student in essence, a third parent (Ogletree 1970).

In public schools, to combat the experience of changing teachers every year, many public-school educators are exploring the concept of *looping,* an idea that has been around since the one-room schoolhouse days. A simple concept, it received favorable attention during the 1990s. According to Grant, Johnson, and Richardson (1996), looping occurs when a teacher stays with one class for two consecutive years. Grant and his colleagues believe the looping strategy offers several advantages. First, teachers save time at the beginning of the second year, when normally several weeks are needed to become familiar with the children and to review. More important than the time factor, however, is the relationship formed between teacher and students. "Our experience indicates that the most important variable in a positive elementary school program is the constant attention of a single teacher/caregiver with whom the child can develop a predictable and meaningful relationship" (Grant et al. 1996, 15).

Looping also allows stronger partnerships with the parents, as a sense of community is instilled with the parents (family), child(ren), and teacher. Relationships deepen as the teacher remains with the class, allowing teachers to grow with and more deeply understand their students. The strong child–teacher–parent bond also helps everyone work though problems instead of handing them on to a different teacher the following year. Some may view the eight-year Waldorf cycle as extreme; however, the benefits teachers experience from the two-year looping arrangements can be extended when teachers remain with their classes for an even longer period of time. Continuity, trust, and meaningful relationships are qualities often lacking in our schools today. One of the greatest benefits of looping is the opportunity for kids to develop a loving, trusting relationship with an adult.

Curriculum and Instruction. Another essential element of any school is the curriculum and instruction used in the classroom. The curriculum and instruction in most of today's public schools is driven by state and national standards and high-stakes testing created by people who typically have no connection with the school. Knowledge is conceptualized as a product, students are viewed as human capital, and instruction is seen as a problem of management. Reading, mathematics, and writing are often emphasized over reflective thinking, substantive content, and artistic and musical creativity. Teachers in many conventional schools have been stripped of their creativity and limited to managing prepackaged instructional programs; they must "teach to the test" and are then held accountable for their students' success, measured only by state-mandated achievement tests. According to Steven Wolk's (2007) scathing article on the current state of public schools:

We are living in a schooling delusion. Do we really believe that our schools inspire our children to live a life of thoughtfulness, imagination, empathy, and social responsibility?... We dumb down and sanitize the curriculum in the name of techno-rational efficiency and "American interests." (p. 649)

He goes on to say that children's schooling consists mostly of filling in the blanks on worksheets, memorizing and regurgitating facts from textbooks, taking multiple-choice tests, and making the "occasional diorama." Students learn subjects in an isolated manner, spending short blocks of time on one particular topic.

In his bestselling book, *Last Child in the Woods*, Richard Louv (2005) compares such segmented, superficial learning to skimming across the ocean while never realizing that there is something under the surface. Because of this kind of instruction, students do not see the connections among topics, nor do those topics seem real to them. Little time is devoted to exploring subjects in depth, which causes children to learn only isolated facts. This way of teaching does not capture students' attention or speak to their souls.

In Waldorf schools, students do not learn in a fragmentary way, nor is the curriculum prepackaged. Waldorf education employs theme-based instruction through the *main lesson*. The main lesson is taught every morning for approximately two hours and focuses on reading and composition, mathematics, science, history, or geography. If, for example, a fourth-grade class is studying fractions, they will spend two hours each day for three to four weeks on this topic. During the two-hour main lesson, nearly all other areas of the curriculum will be woven into the topic, including music, movement, art, storytelling, drama, and writing. The students thus learn in an integrated, holistic manner (Sturbaum 1997). Steiner was adamant about teaching children a curriculum in which all subjects connect and interweave, with nothing isolated or in a vacuum and every part seen as part of the whole (Reinsmith 1989). "Feeling the whole in every part, children discover how they are knitted right into the fabric of the physical world and its mysteries, right into the world of objects and feelings and doings" (Richards 1980, 76).

In addition to teaching a curriculum that allows students to study a subject deeply, Waldorf schools, from their inception, have offered a curriculum designed to nurture all of the intelligences as defined by Howard Gardner (1983). In a recent television appearance, Gardner noted that Waldorf schools fully embody the notion of multiple intelligences. According to Armstrong (1994), Waldorf education embodies in a truly organic sense all eight of Gardner's intelligences. Eisner (1994, 83) also believes that Waldorf schools "pay ... serious attention to the use of multiple aptitudes and the development of diverse forms of knowing." In most main lessons, children sing, recite verses, move rhythmically, draw, and listen. Since the child is an integrated organism, the body, soul, and spirit must be fully developed. Thus, in addition to the academic subjects, Waldorf schools offer lessons in singing, painting, drawing, eurythmy (artistic or therapeutic movement), instrumental music, physical education, handwork, woodworking, and gardening. By working with the hands and moving with the body, children are given a balance between the academic and the more visual and kinesthetic way of learning (Koetzsch 1989; Ogletree 1974).

Not only is the curriculum balanced, but also the activities of the school day are balanced. There is a certain rhythm and flow to the day that takes into consideration the inner rhythm of the children. Because Steiner believed that "head" learning should be followed by "heart" learning (owing to the physiological demands of intellectual learning and the therapeutic role of the arts), the artistic and physically active subjects are taught during the middle and later parts of the day.

Academic subjects are arranged in a sequence to be compatible with the child's cognitive or psychological development. According to Steiner (2000), this sequence follows the evolution of human consciousness, which in turn parallels the awakening of the child's inner consciousness. For example, in first grade, children learn content through fairy tales; second graders learn through fables and legends of saints. Creation stories are taught in third grade, followed in fourth and fifth grades by Norse myths and Greek mythology. Sixth graders learn about the Middle Ages and Roman times; seventh graders study the Renaissance; and eighth graders study history to the present time.

The subjects are taught using a kinesthetic, artistic approach. Generally, textbooks are not used, except perhaps in the upper grades for mathematics. Teachers develop their own materials and teach content through storytelling and biographies. In addition, teachers make every effort to present academic subjects in ways that involve students artistically, as well as rhythmically, or bodily. Pupils write and illustrate their work in "main-lesson books," which contain examples of their best work and the key concepts learned throughout the main lesson. These books help teachers evaluate student progress and become a valuable resource for showing growth over time. Main-lesson books are actually a "post-Steiner" convention and have no direct link to Steiner's educational work; they represent the way it's done now.

Waldorf schools offer a rich curriculum that engages children in the arts and humanities. Moreover, Waldorf philosophy stresses the importance of teaching to the whole child, loving and respecting each child as an individual. Teachers also teach their students to care for and respect nature as well as one another. The curriculum at a Waldorf school is designed to teach social values, which is accomplished in a truly organic way. Every morning, students recite a verse that honors nature and offers thanks for the day. The stories that students hear each day and throughout the year almost always include moral values, brought to the children through the archetypes often found in the traditional folktales, fairy tales, myths, and legends. These simple tales pose the hero or heroine in a difficult life situation, and then show how major obstacles are overcome through perseverance, honesty, and compassion.

Teachers stress the connection between students and nature, and one with another. Steven Wolk's (2007) article "Why Go to School?" cites what most children today are *not* learning in school: love of learning, caring and empathy, environmental literacy, multicultural community, social responsibility, peace and nonviolent resolution of problems, media literacy, global awareness (not just learning to *compete* in a global economy), the fundamentals of money, family, food, and creativity, and imagination. He calls these topics "schooling for human beings."

Through my work with Waldorf education, Wolk's topics seem very similar to what Rudolf Steiner had in mind when he created the first Waldorf school in 1919. Why not learn from a well-established method of education? Over the years, public education has had a history of jumping on every new bandwagon, rather than exploring what works with children, both past and present. We have found that Waldorf-inspired education does indeed make a difference in the lives of public-school teachers and children. Read on to find out about the history of the Waldorf-inspired Cadre and how they have reaped the benefits of implementing Waldorf-inspired methods in their public-school classrooms.

2

THE WALDORF-INSPIRED CADRE

"My prayer for the world is for all children everywhere to learn to love the Earth, to be taught reverence and respect for nature and one another, to appreciate beauty in music, art, literature, and poetry and to love learning." (Mary Goral)

THE BEGINNING OF 1990s witnessed countless changes and reform efforts in the arena of public schools. The restructuring and reform efforts may reflect attempts of well-meaning educators and politicians to "right" public education before the new millennium, or perhaps it was a continuation of the ever-changing landscape of education in the U.S. Although many of the reforms initiated in the early to mid-1990s fell by the wayside, some innovative and creative programs and projects remain and have grown in spite of the current environment of national standards and high-stakes testing.

How do we create a program for teachers that goes beyond the day-to-day functions of public education, one outside the box or where there is no box—a program in which teachers and students grow together, where teaching is inspiring, engaging, and inspired and the whole child is immersed in learning? How do we find or create and sustain such a program?

One such program exists in Louisville, Kentucky, as the Jefferson County Public Schools (JCPS) Waldorf-inspired Cadre, also known as the Waldorf-inspired Project. Initiated by Caroline Pinné, a retired coordinator of JCPS Curriculum Resource Center, the Waldorf-inspired Cadre consists of public-school teachers who have agreed to go on a journey, take risks, and learn new skills along with their students. Introduced to Waldorf education in 1988 by Janey Newton (cofounder of the Waldorf School of Louisville [WSL]), it was a collaborative dream of Janey and Caroline to bring some form of Waldorf education into the public schools. As a lifelong public school educator, Caroline recognized the value and importance of Waldorf methods and practices.

> We went to Cincinnati and visited the Waldorf school...and went to several sessions where Waldorf educators spoke to that faculty. I remember one speaker who talked about social studies and relating historical content through stories and biography.... I was enthralled by the story, the way it was told...and we were given some artistic things to do.... And I thought, "Oh, I like this. I like this idea that there can be something that is so very alive." (personal interview)

A committee was formed to study the possibility of bringing a private Waldorf school to Louisville. They read several books on Waldorf education and had many discussions. Some of the educational aspects resonated with Caroline: "As a teacher, I really believed students needed to be engaged...that they need to have some type of authentic application to what they were studying" (personal interview). As a former public-school teacher, Caroline had always infused the arts into her teaching, but in a haphazard manner. Through her introduction to Waldorf education, she started to envision how the arts could be integrated in a much more holistic manner and how this type of learning could be engaging for students.

In early 1994, Janey Newton gave something to Caroline that was much more powerful than either ever suspected. It was a beautiful poster of the Waldorf education curriculum that gave a holistic view of the curricular themes and infused artistic elements. Caroline displayed the poster in the Curriculum Resource Center (CRC) and a teacher from the public schools, Mary Holden, who frequented the CRC, saw the poster and became very excited.

Janey informed Caroline the same year about a new program at Rudolf Steiner College that featured Waldorf methods applied in the public schools. Rudolf Steiner College had worked with the Sacramento city schools and their title 1 program and decided to bring a two-week institute to public-school teachers. They designed the institute to help public-school educators integrate Waldorf-inspired teaching into their classrooms. With funding from Janey Newton, Caroline, Mary Holden, and Peggy Bahr (both elementary teachers) attended the institute during that inaugural summer in 1994. According to Caroline, she did not initially take to the teaching methods.

> We were marching around the room…. They did not seem to want to talk to you about what they were doing…. And then it came time to paint…and everyone groaned…. But the manner that they used in the painting, that they started us painting with just exploring color…it was so beautiful. And the effect was phenomenal because it wasn't just painting; it was learning about color, how color interacts together. There was also this very calming aspect that balanced the anxiety I was feeling. (personal interview)

By the second week, Caroline could apprehend the purpose of the activities and pedagogy. She began to see beyond what her instructors were saying, how everything they did could be used to build community in the classroom, and how storytelling and painting worked together to create a deeper meaning to the subject matter. The three Kentuckians returned, filled with excitement and personally and professionally renewed, ready to share their newfound knowledge. They offered workshops during the fall of 1994 and in the spring of 1995. Public- and private-school teachers were thrilled with the workshops and immediately went back to their classrooms and tried methods such as the morning circle, which includes rhythmic movement, poetry, and singing. They gave Caroline positive feedback, and she decided it was worth exploring more deeply. How could they integrate these elements of Waldorf education into the public-school mandates?

Caroline was further inspired by participants' comments, such as the following from the first summer institute:

> This was undoubtedly one of the finest educational experiences I have ever had. I felt that so much of my own potential was opened up in areas that I would not have expected. It was marvelous to see how all of the activities were intertwined and supported each other. And it was beautiful to see how others as well as myself had the experience of hidden and unexpected talents blossoming and new interests awakening. This is definitely the way we should be teaching. The program was a marvelously coherent whole. (Robert Jamison, Ph.D., Professor of Mathematics, Clemson University)

Caroline began to think of like-minded teachers who had attended the workshops during the 1994–1995 school year, and who might be interested in attending the institute in California the next summer. She looked to educators involved in the arts and to those who instinctively oriented their teaching toward the whole child. Caroline also knew she would need financial support for the project. Continued collaboration with Janey Newton garnered the beginning financial support through Janey's Creative Education Foundation. The purpose of the foundation was to build a cadre of JCPS teachers who could infuse Waldorf-inspired educational methods into their classrooms. Louisville is blessed to have the support of several foundations that support the arts, in particular projects connected with Waldorf education. Caroline's grant was approved and she quickly recruited interested teachers in the district who would accompany her to California to attend the public-school institute. Caroline, along with nine public-school teachers, made the trek to Rudolf Steiner College during summer 1995. Since that summer, the Waldorf-inspired Cadre has grown and changed, both in dimension and personnel. It has continued to receive the support in the form of grant funding from the Norton

Foundation (Janey Newton's family foundation). The following pages describe the journey of the Cadre; how it has grown and changed, and most importantly, the nature of its sustainability.

THE EARLY YEARS (1995 TO 1998)

Ten Louisvillians attended the two-week Rudolf Steiner College Waldorf in the Public School Institute and were awakened to a new way of teaching and learning. As learners, they experienced the rhythm and balance provided by the Waldorf educational curriculum through music and movement, storytelling and poetry, form drawing, painting, and handwork. They found themselves spontaneously singing through the day, marveling at their accomplishments with knitting or playing the recorder and enjoying their growth as painters and artists.

Upon their return, Caroline wrote the following:

> After two weeks of active immersion in experiential learning, we feel forever changed in how we comprehend the learning process. The Waldorf educational approach deftly weaves the academics and the arts into an aesthetic tapestry of depth and richness. The needs of the learner, not an organization, are the focus of curriculum and experience. Child development and the phrase "developmentally appropriate" now have more form and substance for us.

Teachers agreed to meet once a month during the following school year to reconnect with their Waldorf colleagues and share their enthusiasm for the unfolding of teaching-learning partnerships in their classrooms. Ongoing, organized opportunities to meet and discuss the effects of new learning/teaching are essential to effective professional development. Together, teachers explored their efforts in applying Waldorf-inspired educational approaches with their students, and reaffirmed their commitment to nurture daily the young people in their charge.

Caroline worked with the Cadre as facilitator, encourager, and connector. A key ingredient of successful professional development is to have the so-called experts right in your own backyard. In other words, rather than gathering teachers together for a full day, a one-shot deal of "sit and get" from an outside guru, local "key" people are regularly available to answer questions, offer support, and ongoing training. Not only did the Cadre meet monthly, they also offered workshops for fellow teachers. During the 1995-96 school year, Caroline and two Cadre members presented "Rhythm, Storytelling, and Art—A Waldorf-inspired Approach" at a conference sponsored by the Greater Louisville Council of the International Reading Association. Professional development is also more successful if it can be sustained by instructing those in an organization to teach their colleagues. In addition to staff development, Caroline also brought in well-known Waldorf educators from around the country to speak with interested teachers and administrators.

Even during that first school year, Cadre members brought amazing things to their classrooms. One teacher introduced Norse myths to her fourth graders, performed the play "Idunn and the Apples of Youth," held festivals, taught recorder, painted using the wet-on-wet technique, and created main-lesson books. Another Cadre member maintained a nature table in her kindergarten and filled the classroom with silk scarves and wooden structures for play. A fifth-grade teacher taught juggling, cross-stitch, weaving, and clay sculpture to his students. One particular elementary school received a two-thousand-dollar grant to extend Waldorf-inspired educational experiences in their classrooms.

As Caroline visited Cadre members' classrooms, she witnessed students mature in poise and confidence through singing in rounds and playing the recorder, and noted that several older students who would normally never reveal any part of themselves became transformed artists who shared their acquired knowledge and skills through in-class performances.

After the first year's introduction to implementing Waldorf-inspired methods into their classrooms, six of the nine teachers agreed to return to California to the two-week summer institute at Rudolf Steiner College. Before leaving for California, Caroline wrote the following:

Wrapping themselves in the stories of their classrooms and with insatiable inquisitiveness, six of these teachers will return for the second year sessions this summer. With continued grant funding and sponsorship, administrative support, and teachers wanting a more balanced learning experience that unfolds the uniqueness within each student, the potential is wonderfully blooming in our educational community.

The Project Grows in Form and Function

The 1996–1997 school year witnessed growth of the Cadre project in a number of areas. Caroline's Curriculum Resource Center began a library of Waldorf educational materials, and the mailing list grew to fifty-one people. Teachers who had attended the 1996 summer institute again offered workshops to colleagues. Caroline, with the help of The Creative Education Foundation, created an application process in grant funding for teachers who wanted to attend the public-school institute in Sacramento. In return for the training grant, teachers were expected to fulfill certain responsibilities, including the following:

1. Implement Waldorf-inspired methods and experiences appropriate to your classroom program
2. Act as a member of an advisory group that will plan and present workshops, demonstrations, and discussion groups concerned with Waldorf education
3. Participate in the activities planned by the advisory group
4. Share the responsibility in planning, creating, and maintaining an ongoing display and resource area in the Curriculum Resource Center
5. Design and implement a format in which you can share your experiences with the Waldorf-inspired training and its effects in your classroom (i.e., presenting a workshop, creating a display, action-research project, classroom exchange, and so forth).

Teachers were also asked to evaluate their experience at the summer institute in California. The comments of teachers who attended were poignant and revealing. A few of those evaluations follow.

> In my experience, I see a great need for public-school children to be influenced by a sense of calmness and inner peace.... Many pressures such as poverty, violence, and broken families contribute to the inability of children to achieve academic success. I have seen children respond to a rich aesthetic environment, which is a central principle of Waldorf education. I am convinced that the Waldorf-inspired program will enrich my students' lives in many ways. (Laura Blankenbaker 1996)

A high-school teacher who worked with underachieving students, wrote the following:

> No longer do I hold to "tried and true" methods; my new motto is, if it doesn't engage the student, if it doesn't empower him/her to accomplish something beyond that moment, *then don't do it!* Waldorf-inspired education and our program are a perfect match. (Denise Jensen 1996)

As noted, the Cadre again offered workshops to fellow teachers in their school district. The first session took place at the 1996 Early Literacy Institute, where they presented "Art, Rhythm, and Storytelling." Interestingly, this workshop drew some rather sharp criticism from thirteen out of ninety participants. Some thought the presentation was too "new age," others did not like the idea of chanting to movements. Still others noted that Steiner and Waldorf Education were on a "list" of occult programs against Christianity.

As a result of this sharp criticism, Caroline decided the project needed to be infused with current educational research and began looking to brain research and Gardner's (1983) theory of multiple intelligences to back up the teachings inherent in Waldorf education. From that point on, the workshops and meetings were framed with questions, titles, and goals connected with the mission and language of public education. An example from a 1996 flier from Jefferson

County Public Schools Institutes and Special Program appeared as follows:

Integrating the Arts with Waldorf Education

Waldorf Education emphasizes an integrated arts approach to education. Of particular interest to public-school educators are the techniques of movement, music, art, handwork, poetry and storytelling that can be used as tools for student success.... During the school year the Curriculum Resource Center will schedule a series of workshop experiences featuring 1) identification of the elements of Waldorf Education that inspire the learning process; 2) correlation with KERA (Kentucky Education Reform Act) and the multiple-intelligences theory; 3) integration of arts and academics with classroom examples; and 4) an illustration of how Waldorf-inspired methods meet the needs of diverse learners.

The more grounded approach to the workshops seemed to alleviate criticisms from participants. Many teachers commented on a desire to learn more about the multiple-intelligence theory and nearly all stated a desire to learn more about Waldorf-inspired methods.

That year, Caroline also received a grant from the school district for six Cadre members to visit the Urban Waldorf School in Milwaukee, the first public Waldorf school in the United States. The school-district grant paid for travel, and an additional grant from the Norton Foundation paid for substitutes for the traveling teachers. The purpose of this visit was to explore how the Urban Waldorf School implemented the Waldorf curriculum, how they structured their day, what methods they used, the design of the physical environment, and how the school integrated district expectations and goals into their own philosophy and vision.

Following the visit to Milwaukee, the team was inspired to bring more Waldorf-inspired education to Louisville. Caroline wrote in her 1996–1997 grant request to the Creative Arts Foundation, "I feel that the Waldorf-inspired Project is at a significant threshold. To build on these last two years and bring a significant depth to the JCPS Waldorf-inspired project will require additional funding and assistance." In the grant proposal were several recommendations on how to grow the project. Some of those recommendations are included below:

- Conduct a qualitative research project in collaboration with the University of Louisville and the JCPS Waldorf Cadre
- Explore requirements and support for a Waldorf school in JCPS
- Provide a three-to-four day Institute in Louisville for the summer of 1997
- Explore the possibilities for further in-depth Waldorf training and certification
- Design and produce a video
- Produce writings regarding the JCPS Waldorf in the Public Schools Project
- Identify current curriculum that is compatible with the Waldorf-inspired approach
- Connect Waldorf methodologies with KERA, multiple intelligences, constructivist models, inquiry-based learning, whole language, and thematic instruction

Caroline also included in the 1996 to 1997 grant a proposal to fund Mary Holden to assist with the project. Mary, one of the first Cadre members who attended the public-school institute in California, was on sabbatical from teaching and wanted to do research on the project and include a number of the above recommendations in her work. Specifically, Mary and Caroline included the following in their proposal:

- Assist the CRC coordinator in planning and developing a multi-day institute in the summer of 1997
- Develop and produce workshop handouts, formats, and examples with a multicultural emphasis
- Produce a quarterly publication about the JCPS Waldorf in the Public Schools Project
- Design and produce videos related to the JCPS Waldorf in the Public Schools Project

- Identify and correlate current curriculum that is compatible with the Waldorf inspired approach, to include a more updated, multicultural perspective with a wider variance in stories and poetry, mathematics-problem solving, and the writing process
- Develop and organize files, displays, and an annotated bibliography of Waldorf materials in the CRC
- Assist teachers in the JCPS Waldorf in the Public Schools Cadre

That year, Mary and Caroline accomplished many of the above projects. Mary kept copious notes at the monthly Cadre meetings, many with vignettes on children's learning that will be shared in following chapters. The quarterly newsletter featured upcoming dates of Cadre events, as well as informative writings about Waldorf education in general and specific happenings in Cadre teachers' classrooms. Caroline wrote in the October issue:

> Weaving the arts into daily practice allows the learners to engage in diverse practices that not only develop unique gifts, but strengthen areas that need development. Waldorf education structures the learning process to meet the developmental needs of the whole child through a curriculum that balances the sciences, humanities, and the arts.

Mary created a handout for the festivals celebrated in a Waldorf school and blended this beautifully with festivals celebrated around the world. Three after-school workshops were offered in the fall, including one for middle- and high-school teachers entitled "Enriching Learning through Movement and Recitation"; one for elementary teachers, focusing on math, called "Active Learning with Music and Rhythm"; and a handwork session for anyone interested. The Waldorf in the Public Schools discussion group continued to meet the second Monday of each month where they entertained issues such as connections to current research on learning and the role of poetry and biography in the classroom.

For those people new to Waldorf education, the Waldorf-inspired Cadre offered a workshop entitled "Introduction to Waldorf in the

Public Schools." At this particular workshop, attendees received eight pieces of literature, ranging from newspaper articles to journal publications, all of which backed up the use of Waldorf educational methods in public and private schools. Teachers new to Waldorf education and the Waldorf in the Public Schools Project were added to the mailing list, bringing the total to 139.

Betty Staley visited in January of 1997 and offered a day-long workshop for teachers entitled "Waldorf Education: Change, Constancy, and Traditions—Deepening Conceptual Knowledge through the Arts, Rhythm, and Language."

As mentioned, a group of Cadre members met each month to deepen their understanding of Waldorf education. During the winter of 1997, participants read excerpts from A. C. Harwood's *The Recovery of Man in Childhood* and were asked to write reflections on their readings. This more in-depth study intended to help further teachers' knowledge of child development, a key to Waldorf education. Other monthly sessions included a study of the main lesson, discussion of the Waldorf curriculum, and an overview of the JCPS Waldorf Cadre video.

The video project, "Weaving Academics and the Arts throughout the Curriculum: Adapting Waldorf Educational Methods in JCPS Classrooms," intended to showcase and demonstrate what teachers could not see at workshops, such as children using Waldorf methods, their interactions, and comments.

The continuation of the newsletter also helped inform teachers about upcoming Waldorf events. The March issue told of three workshops: one featured singing games, a knitting workshop, and a day-long workshop in June with Waldorf educator Liz Bevens. The May 1997 issue featured an article by Caroline, urging teachers to renew and refresh themselves during the summer.

> As educators, we feel our energy depleted, our commitment to excellence withered, and our inner being parched. Who will push us to that reservoir that replenishes the very core of our being? How can we tap that part of ourselves that rejuvenates

a new sense of self-autonomy, resilience, expectancy, and excitement?

Attending the Waldorf Methods in the Public Schools summer institute was one way to accomplish this renewal. During the summer of 1997 eight people from Louisville made their way to Sacramento for another summer of life-changing and enhancing educational experiences.

By September 1997, the Cadre had grown to twenty-three members. In order to effectively keep in touch with the members, Caroline used e-mail as well as the U.S. Postal Service for correspondence. Because teachers are so inundated with paperwork, Caroline also sent follow-up messages as well. In addition, she made individual phone calls to Cadre members prior to events. This type of follow-through is essential when building a program and sustaining a successful professional-development agenda.

The agenda for the 1997–1998 school year proved to be quite full for teachers in the Waldorf-inspired Cadre. Monthly meetings were held in which the group alternated between sharing sessions and skills development. During the September meeting, Cadre members decided on the agenda for the year, plans for district-wide workshops, and visitation with paid professional-leave days to one another's classrooms, as well as to the Waldorf School of Louisville. The group also listed wishes, concerns, and issues relating to the integration of Waldorf-inspired methods into their classrooms. Furthermore, in keeping with the previous year's commitment to connect Waldorf education with current educational research, Cadre members were asked to reflect on the following questions: "How does Waldorf education increase reading, writing, and mathematics competency in my classroom?" And "What can I use as evidence of progress with specific students in literacy learning, social skills, participation, quality, and persistence of work?"

Betty Staley returned in January 1998 and presented a session entitled "Waldorf Education: The Teacher as Artist and Mentor—Enhancing the Learning Process for Each Student through an Arts-filled Curriculum." Not only did Betty present the work-shop, she also visited Cadre members' classrooms and met with them to follow up and answer questions. Ongoing mentoring is crucial for successful professional development. According to Wood, Thompson, and Russell (1981), new professional behaviors are not permanent, even when they become part of a teacher's or a class's ongoing activi-ties. By providing systematic mentoring, teachers have the opportu-nity to reflect, garner support and feedback, and gain confidence in their implementation of new methods and ideas.

Interestingly, my first introduction to the Louisville's Waldorf-inspired Cadre was at this session. At the time I was a professor at Hanover College, a small liberal-arts institution "across the river" in southern Indiana. A colleague informed me of Betty Staley's presenta-tion, as she knew of my work with Waldorf education and my keen interest in Waldorf methods applied in the public-school setting. I introduced myself to Betty after her presentation and she invited me to come to Rudolf Steiner College for the public school institute in the summer of 1998. But I'm jumping ahead of myself—there is still much to tell about the Cadre's story for the remainder of the 1997–1998 school year.

After Betty's January visit, Caroline asked the Cadre to reflect on the impact Betty's sessions made on them as educators and how their educational choices were influenced or altered. Caroline realized the importance of reflection as a critical function of successful teaching and learning. Nearly one-hundred years ago, John Dewey (1910) characterized reflection as a process of sense-making that arose out of a felt need, usually in the form of an open-ended question about student learning or pedagogy. This connection of the teaching/learning process led Betty to suggest to Caroline that the teachers might begin reading some introductory lectures by Rudolf Steiner, and offered "Human Values in Education," a lecture delivered in Holland in 1924 as a possible first choice. Betty felt it was time for the Cadre members to begin connecting Waldorf methods to the theory behind the practice. However, Caroline decided to bring Rene Querido's book *Creativity in Education* as an alternative. Bridging the gap between public education and Rudolf Steiner's philosophic works was something Caroline was reluctant to do. Given recent unsuccessful litigation in the state of California against the Waldorf charter schools (1997–2005), it was wise to continue bringing Waldorf education through its effective arts-based methods.

Monthly meetings continued throughout the second semester. Yet due to the increased nature of teacher responsibilities in JCPS, it appeared that several events had to be rescheduled or postponed. However, Cadre members were able to offer two workshops in March, one for elementary teachers entitled "Re-energize Your Classroom: Movement and Academic Success—A Waldorf-inspired Workshop at the Elementary Level" and the second for middle- and high-school teachers called "Re-energize your Curriculum through a Waldorf-inspired Approach." Both workshops were well attended and teachers rated the sessions quite highly.

Spring of 1998 also saw another attempt at producing a research project by an outside consultant. Caroline began working on funding for this and it appears that some progress was made, but it did not result in a completed project. Funding was also sought for the following school year from the Norton Foundation to continue the Waldorf-inspired Project and to send nine JCPS teachers to the Waldorf Methods in the Public Schools Institute at Rudolf Steiner College during the summer of 1998.

Teachers were also invited to attend a local three-day workshop given by Liz Bevins, a Waldorf educator from the Sacramento Waldorf School. The purpose of this workshop was to help JCPS Cadre teachers refine what they had learned in California, assist them in examining their beliefs and practices about using the Waldorf-inspired approach in the public schools, and integrate Waldorf concepts into the JCPS standards and curriculum. Twelve people attended the sessions and many referred to the JCPS core content (new standards for the school district) in their evaluations and how they intended to relate Waldorf practices to that document. Interestingly, the 1997–1998 school year was the first to mention standards—definitely a precursor of what was to come.

THE MIDDLE YEARS (1998 TO 2003)

As with all innovative projects, the initial enthusiasm wears off and the reality of the hard work involved sets in. Leadership often changes, requiring others to take up the work or to work "under the radar." Although JCPS hired a new superintendent about the same time the Cadre project began, this person's hardcore ideas on curriculum and teaching did not really begin to affect teachers until he had been there for a few years. One must also take into consideration the changing political climate in the U.S. and the unfortunate introduction of the No Child Left Behind legislation. The Standards movement was in full swing, with the National Council of Teachers of Mathematics (NCTM) leading the way. NCTM Curriculum and Evaluation Standards were published in 1998, and other academic subject areas soon followed with their version of national standards. Although the U.S. did not and has yet to adopt a national curriculum for public schools, our country has definitely put much stock in the national standards for all academic subjects.

Given the cultural changes taking place in the broader educational environment, it is no surprise that the Waldorf-inspired Cadre also experienced some changes. Fortunately the funding was not cut, as was the case for many innovative programs across the country, and luckily Caroline remained at the helm. However, Caroline's duties as director of the Curriculum Resource Center increased, drawing much of her attention away from the Cadre. The yearly notebooks full of meticulous records that she kept about the Waldorf-inspired Project gave way to electronic folders and separate workshop files. Time was not available to continue an aesthetic portfolio of the remaining years of the project, yet the Cadre persevered and continued to bring Waldorf-inspired teaching to their students.

The Waldorf-inspired workshops for JCPS teachers seemed to diminish, as many other directives from the district required teachers to attend school-wide professional development sessions. Unfortunately, a large number of children in Jefferson County were reading below grade level and as a result, JCPS adopted a scripted reading program in hopes that a more standard, systematic approach to teaching reading would help. This mandated reading initiative stripped teachers of their creativity, thus making it much more difficult to integrate Waldorf-inspired methods into their classrooms. Furthermore, all time spent in the classroom had to be accounted for and many teachers were required to turn in weekly plans to their principals. District-wide teams of professionals dropped in on teachers to see if they were following the mandated curriculum.

Nearly all schools in the district adopted standards-based mathematics series, which also required more teacher training, as these curricula were more processed-based and less skills-oriented. With more and more attention placed on testing, teachers and principals were reluctant to try anything out of the ordinary. Principals' jobs were on the line, as a failing school (a school whose students did not perform at a proficient level on the state test), spelled disaster for that principal. With so much pressure on the principal, the trickle-down effect was felt keenly by teachers, and the days of creating one's own lessons seemed to be gone.

Cadre members continued to meet, but not as often, as teachers' time was now spent entering countless preparatory-test scores into computers, for example, and desperately trying to help their students perform well on the test. Meetings and workshops occurred one to two times per semester, and rather than presenting the workshops to fellow teachers, Cadre members seemed to want to sit back and just be fed. Caroline found other people knowledgeable in Waldorf education and brought them in to present workshops for the Cadre. Japa Buckner, a brilliant teacher from the Waldorf School of Louisville, worked tirelessly with Cadre members to help them become more intentional with their integration of Waldorf-inspired teaching.

This intentionality is extremely important for those interested in bringing Waldorf-inspired pedagogy to the public-school setting. Often, when public-school teachers first discover Waldorf education, they see and understand it in only a rather shallow way. This is not a criticism of public-school teachers. For those who have studied Waldorf education and know it deeply, this observation makes perfect sense. However, those new to Waldorf may not understand that everything that happens in a Waldorf school happens for a reason. Newcomers may think that children sing and dance their way through every school day, not knowing that every song and every dance and movement is intended to teach something quite specific. This failure to understand intentionality, coupled with a narrow focus on teaching to the test, required those working with the Cadre to make sure teachers understood why they were doing certain things.

Even with the increased expectations for classroom teachers, the Cadre continued to grow and Caroline was able to send three to four people each year to California to the RSC Waldorf Methods in the Public School Institute. Also of interest were the teams of teachers who came together at a number of elementary schools in the district. Dixie Elementary had a team of four teachers who called themselves the "Dixie Chicks." They supported one another in their integration of Waldorf-inspired methods and were able to do more as a team than as individuals. Another school, Byck Elementary, began a kindergarten-through-fifth-grade Waldorf-inspired team. Students' parents could request that their children be in the Waldorf track, and these kids would then receive a Waldorf-inspired education for their entire elementary career. Two other elementary schools, Lowe and Blue Lick, also attracted two to three Cadre teachers who were able to loop with their students. Although their years looping was not as long as children often experience in a private Waldorf school, even two years with the same teacher helped build stronger communities and in turn relationships that often increased students' love of school and of learning.

Even though Caroline continued working with and supporting the Cadre, she had gotten to the point after the turn of the millennium where she knew she could not take the Waldorf project any further. She began to imagine someone new stepping in and taking the Cadre to the next level. In Caroline's words, "And then this angel, in the form of Mary Goral, moved to Louisville."

FROM 2003 TO 2008

Although I am not an angel, I did have the necessary knowledge and credentials to take the Cadre to the next level. In the fall of 2003, I joined the education faculty at Bellarmine University in Louisville. Bellarmine is a Catholic liberal arts institution with a fine reputation in the area and a history of a social justice mission. Bellarmine also houses the world's largest collection of Thomas Merton's work, and prides itself on the integration of Merton's philosophy into its many classes and seminars. Given Bellarmine's focus and my passion for bringing Waldorf-inspired education to the public-school setting, it was a perfect fit.

Due to my prior work with Waldorf education in the public-school setting, including the creation of a Waldorf-inspired master's program at Mount Mary College in Milwaukee, as well as my tenure as a Waldorf teacher, it was not surprising that Caroline wanted me to take up the work with the Cadre. She felt that tying the Cadre to a university setting would help legitimize the work the teachers were already doing and would also afford the opportunity to take the education of the Cadre further. Caroline was right.

During my first year at Bellarmine, my graduate chair asked me to design a new master's program with an emphasis in Waldorf education. Because my learning curve was fairly steep that year, I did not complete the program design until the following academic year. Rather than create an entirely new master's degree in education, we opted to keep the core courses of our original master's, which consisted of eighteen credit hours (six classes) and use the remaining eighteen elective hours for the Waldorf-inspired courses. This way we would not have to take it to the State Department of Education for approval. I loosely based the six classes on the program we designed in Milwaukee, but did not replicate it exactly, as that program was the intellectual property of Mount Mary College. The procedure for creating the new master's program involved writing course syllabi and descriptions for each class, and then taking those to the university graduate committee. The committee reviewed the proposal and gave the go-ahead for the new master's to begin in the summer of 2005.

Caroline had received grant funding for me to work with the Cadre, and during the first academic year (2003–2004) I presented two workshops and helped lead one retreat. On a glorious Saturday morning in October, we offered "Teaching Mathematics through Literature and the Arts" to over twenty Cadre members. They seemed hungry for new information and for a deeper connection and understanding of Waldorf education. During the three-hour workshop, I told two math stories, taught the teachers math-related poetry and music, and led them through a math-inspired painting. The painting was of the pyramids and could be tied to the state and national standards. That particular standard recommends that students be able to connect a two-dimensional image with a three-dimensional model (see opposite). Throughout the morning, I related everything that we did to the JCPS core content and to Steiner's philosophy of child development.

The next workshop, presented on a Saturday in January, followed a similar format and continued the math-related theme. This time we brought in the handwork teacher from the Urban Waldorf School in Milwaukee, and we worked with the Cadre for the entire day. It is important to note that Cadre members received professional-development credit for every workshop they attended. Because teachers in JCPS are required to earn twenty-four hours of PD credit each year, Cadre teachers were given an extra incentive to attend the workshops. Not only were they fulfilling a district requirement, they were doing something they loved.

In March, Caroline and I planned an overnight retreat at a rustic lodge in a nearby state park. We focused this retreat on science and worked hard on creating stories, songs, poetry, and artwork that helped the teachers bring the difficult concepts they were required to teach to the children in a more developmentally appropriate manner. Kathleen O'Laughlin, the handwork teacher from Milwaukee, came again and knitted animals with the teachers and Jennifer Geroski, Cadre member, presented singing games. Spending an extended amount of time

A math-inspired painting

with one another helped strengthen bonds and renew friendships. It was a wonderful experience.

During the summer of 2004, I offered a three-day workshop on the Waldorf history curriculum, but it was not well attended. Caroline and I understood that teachers were in need of rest and renewal, and that the summer workshop really should be replaced with the graduate institute. Luckily, that was to take place the following summer.

The 2004-5 academic year saw tremendous growth for the Waldorf-inspired project. As previously mentioned, this was the year that the master's program was written, approved and implemented. We also offered two workshops in the fall of 2004, both with a focus on social studies. The first was entitled "Weaving Literacy into Social Studies" and the second "Growth of Culture and Freedom in the United States." As in the previous academic year, the workshops included singing, poetry, movement, storytelling, and artwork. These particular sessions featured biographies, spirituals, and handwork. Again, the JCPS core content and more in-depth information on the Waldorf history curriculum were woven into both workshops.

That January, the Cadre presented a showcase of their work. Nearly all of the active Cadre members shared something representative of the work they were doing with the children in their classes. It was truly amazing. From leading songs and poetry in the circle to a guided writing experience on elements of design, the Cadre teachers brilliantly wove together Waldorf-inspired methods with the required content of their disciplines.

In March we were again blessed with a visit from Betty Staley. It had been a few years since Betty had been with the Cadre, and spending time with her helped boost the teachers' lagging spirits, as her visit coincided with the crazy time leading up to the CAT (Commonwealth Achievement Test). Betty led an informal workshop with Cadre teachers on Friday, and on Saturday she presented a more formal workshop on Waldorf-inspired methods. We held the Saturday workshop at Bellarmine and invited interested teachers, administrators, and parents.

In addition, it was now time for the grant that Caroline had received from the Norton Foundation since 1998 to be passed to me. I wish it had been as easy as passing a torch. Since the JCPS Waldorf-inspired Project was actually a part of the Curriculum Resource Center, negotiations began with JCPS, Bellarmine, and the Norton Foundation to move the project to Bellarmine. Through careful planning and dialogue, the project was successfully transferred with all parties in agreement. Writing a grant to a well-established foundation is an incredibly time-consuming process. I began working on the grant in December and after many drafts, turned it in at the beginning of March. Finding out in early April that my first large grant of $39,000 had been approved was a joyous occasion for me.

Although the first summer institute was not to start until late June, I had been preparing for it throughout the academic year. Queries regarding the new Waldorf program increased during the spring, and by meeting with people and answering each phone call and e-mail personally, I began to see the need for Waldorf-teacher training as well as the master's program. A number of teachers in the Cadre had completed their master's as well as their Rank One (thirty credit hours beyond a master's degree), and they wanted to gain more in-depth knowledge about Waldorf education, including Steiner's spiritual science, Anthroposophy. Other people in the community and the surrounding area were interested in taking the Waldorf training because they were teaching in Waldorf schools or wanted eventually to teach in a Waldorf school. So our original idea of a Waldorf-inspired master's program grew into a Waldorf-teacher training with classes that both degree- and non-degree-seeking students could participate in. We offered the non-degree courses through the School of Continuing and Professional Studies. In addition, those teachers who already held a master's degree were interested in taking the classes for credit toward their Rank One. This option was incorporated as well as part of the three-year program (see appendix 2; also www.foxhollowwaldorf.com and www. bellarmine.edu/education/waldorf.asp).

I soon found out that in order for our teacher training to be accredited by the Association of Waldorf Schools of North America (AWSNA), we needed to create a separate entity not tied to an institution (Bellarmine). After a bit of research, we decided to create a nonprofit center for Anthroposophy, which we named Kentahten (Native American for Kentucky, translated as "land of tomorrow"). We also asked Rudolf Steiner College to be our mentor college and they agreed. Part of our association with Rudolf Steiner College includes visiting instructors from the RSC who come to Louisville for two intensives during the three-year program, and a fourth summer wherein our students seeking Waldorf certification attend a specially designed program at the RSC.

With the bulk of this in place, we began our first summer institute. Classes were offered in eurythmy, singing, child development, and teaching science, as well as an evening seminar that featured an introduction to Anthroposophy. Instructors came from Wisconsin, our local Waldorf school, and Bellarmine. Nearly thirty students attended the first two-week institute. Public-school teachers, private-school teachers, parents, and administrators all learned together. It was wildly successful in spite of a number of glitches. On the final day of the intensive, we held our plenum as well as a performance featuring music, movement, poetry, and artwork. Our graduate chair who attended the program commented that this was the purest, most "real" learning experience he had experienced at Bellarmine—ever.

During the 2005–2006 academic year, we offered two anthroposophic study courses through Kentahten Teacher Training, one each semester. The night of our first class was like old home week. Many strong friendships had formed during the summer institute, and it was wonderful coming together after a two-month hiatus. The first workshop of the 2005-6 school year carried the same energy. In September we offered "Weaving the Arts into the Academics," which included eurythmy, handwork, singing, and poetry. The November workshop was on "Games that Teach." Nearly twenty Cadre members and guests attended each first-semester event. In January, we brought in Michael Imes from Milwaukee and Rob Lanier from the Waldorf School of Louisville to do a half-day workshop on form drawing and singing.

In March 2006, we branched out a bit and invited David Sobel, educator and author of numerous books on children and the environment, including *Place Based Education* and *Beyond Ecophobia*. David offered a Friday-night lecture and a Saturday workshop. Both events were open to the public and we had more than thirty excited participants. It is important to note that every workshop we offer is free of charge.

It is worth noting the shift from Cadre members presenting workshops in the early days of the project to bringing in outside consultants to do the presentations. It is clearly a challenge for those of us who are local to continue bringing new material to our group. By bringing in outside consultants who are paid through our grant, we have been able to keep the workshops fresh and interesting for both new and long-time Cadre members.

Speaking of the grant, I had to resubmit the grant proposal to the Norton Foundation in February 2006. I asked for more money the second year ($46,000), in order to bring in more outside consultants and purchase more supplies for Cadre members. One fortunate aspect of the grant is the funding of art materials for Cadre teachers, which include the high-quality supplies found in a Waldorf school. Teachers are asked to fill out an application form for supplies and must commit to presenting at the annual showcase. I found out in April 2006 that the entire amount of the grant request was approved.

As the 2005–2006 academic year drew to a close, I was busy organizing the second year of our summer institute. Again, we had a number of inquiries about the program. Luckily, Louisville is small enough that people interested in Waldorf training are all directed to me. Using a hands-on approach helps keep confusion down and the number of participants up. I meet personally with all new applicants. I do this for a number of reasons. First, I need to find out how much they know about Waldorf education. I give those people new to Waldorf articles to read and ask that they fill out an application for the training (see www.bellarmine.edu/education/waldorf.asp). Second, I find that meeting with people face to face establishes a relationship that could not take place via phone or e-mail: amazing what the personal touch can do.

Classes offered in our institute's second summer included eurythmy, singing, Teaching Mathematics in the Waldorf School, and Art I. The art class featured handwork, woodworking, clay, form drawing, chalkboard drawing, and painting. Again, we brought in instructors from Wisconsin and from the Waldorf School of Louisville. More than thirty people attended and the richness of the two weeks filled everyone to the brim. I find that people in this area of the country are extremely grateful for opportunities that those on the east or west coast often take for granted. Many participants spoke of how "blown away" they were that we had Waldorf-teacher training in Louisville. The new people who joined us during year two were deeply touched by the inclusive nature of the core group. The way the program is set up allows for people to jump into the training at any time. This keeps the training healthy and the numbers of people strong.

Fall 2006 brought torrential rains to the Louisville area and one such storm that dropped six inches of rain in less than an hour coincided with our first workshop of the school year. Chet Celenza, my dear friend and colleague from Prairie Hill Waldorf School in Pewaukee, Wisconsin, arrived in between thunderstorms to present an awesome workshop entitled "Folk Dancing and Global Music." Unfortunately, many people could not attend due to closed roads and flooded basements. However, those who did make it, experienced a high-energy morning, full of new songs, dances, and information. In November, Rob Lanier and Neal Kennerk from our Waldorf school presented the workshop "Art through the Seasons." Rob, a vocalist, introduced new seasonal songs and poems, and Neal, an artist who also taught in the summer institute, worked with teachers on chalk drawing.

In January 2007, the Cadre members offered another showcase of their work. Fifteen Cadre members presented that day. From leading circle activities to discussing and sharing an astronomy block complete with a main-lesson book, the morning session included an impressive display of the teachers' commitment to a Waldorf-inspired education for their students. Several people outside the Cadre attended the morning session as well, and their comments on the teachers' presentations helped to reinforce my passion for bringing Waldorf-inspired education to the public schools.

Shortly after the January showcase, I set about resubmitting our grant proposal to the Norton Foundation. Again, I asked for additional funding. The year's increase included more scholarship money for degree as well as non-degree students, and extra funding to bring in instructors from Rudolf Steiner College. The scholarships are a significant aspect to the success of the program. Bellarmine is a private university, and tuition is nearly twice that of the public institutions in the area. Furthermore, loan and grant monies are not available for students seeking a Rank One. By offering scholarships to graduate students that pay for nearly half their tuition, we are able to attract a number of interested and dedicated teachers who would otherwise be unable to attend. However, the scholarships are not handed out to anyone who is interested. Students are required to fill out an application that is then reviewed by a three-member committee (see appendix 5).

We had scheduled Betty Staley's visit for April 2007, but unfortunately she was unable to come. After our initial disappointment wore off, I redirected my efforts to the planning of the third summer institute. The summer of 2007 proved to be extremely full. Classes included instruction in eurythmy, singing, recorder and flute. We also offered

Teaching Language Arts in the Waldorf School, Art II, and an evening course on the Temperaments. The art class featured instruction in block and stick-crayon drawing, colored-pencil drawing, charcoal drawing, perspective drawing, painting, and games. We brought in Howard Schrager, author of *LMNOP* and veteran Waldorf teacher from California; Mary Ruud from Milwaukee; Rob Lanier and Neal Kennerk from the WSL; Bill Goral (physical-education teacher and husband); and Donna Stottman—long-time Cadre member and master teacher. Each summer I direct the institute and teach as well.

As in the previous years, approximately thirty people attended the two-week intensive. For some students, this was their last summer with our institute, as their fourth summer would be spent at the RSC in Sacramento. Having a solid core of seasoned students helped make this institute even better than the previous two. There was a depth to it that had not been there before. Students made comments such as: "We were taken to a deeper level with the material this year." "The institute seemed better organized than last year. Enjoyed the discussion/lectures." "Dr. Goral is a superb organizer, facilitator, and negotiator for just the right instructors, bringing ideas to practice, demonstration, and participation." "Dr. Goral's skills as collaborator, teacher, and director created a caring, yet academic atmosphere for the two weeks." It will be odd not to have them in our midst during subsequent years. Perhaps they will agree to come back and teach for us.

Our fall and winter schedules for the 2008 academic year was set and student interest high. The fall course, Teaching History and Multicultural Education in the Waldorf School, had a record number of students enrolled and many committed to attending the second-semester class Teaching Geography in the Waldorf School. Our anthroposophic study for the year was Steiner's classic *Outline of Esoteric Science*. It is important to note that not all of our students participate in the Anthroposophy courses. Granted, the study of Anthroposophy is important for a deep understanding of the developing human, but we contend that teachers who bring even a fraction of Waldorf education to their students are doing a greater service than those who include no Waldorf practices at all.

CONCLUSION

This story on the creation and subsequent implementation of bringing Waldorf-inspired pedagogy to the public-school setting holds a number of key ingredients essential for any successful professional-development program. In addition, the Waldorf-inspired Cadre Project contains elements found only in select programs throughout the country. The features that nearly all long-term adult-learning programs have in common include: a readiness to learn coupled with a shared group interest; strong leadership; planning and clear focus; fiscal support; commitment from top leadership; ongoing training and education; long-term commitment; maintenance; and ongoing reflection and evaluation (Wood, Thompson, and Russell 1981; Darling-Hammond 2005). The uncommon ingredient is that of an attention on the inner life of the teacher. Proponents of Parker Palmer's Courage to Teach program relate that "Evoking the inner life of the teacher—that is, engaging teachers in activities that cultivate their capacity to teach with greater consciousness, self-awareness, and integrity—is a necessary condition for successful professional development" (Intrator and Kunzman 2006, 39). This being said, recognizing the common elements of a strong professional-development program also helps one understand the success as well as the longevity of the Waldorf-inspired Project.

Readiness. First and foremost, there was a readiness and a desire to have the program implemented into the public-school system in Louisville. Teachers were hungry for new ideas and the reform effort of the 1990s was in full swing across the country and in the state of Kentucky. During the same time span, the Urban Waldorf School began in Milwaukee and the Waldorf charter movement blossomed on the West Coast.

Leadership. Caroline Pinné is the epitome of a strong leader. She is organized, visionary, resourceful, intelligent, politically savvy, well-connected, hard working, and persistent. She was able to make her vision a reality—something that not everyone can do. Her dedication to the development of the program as well as continued support and interest have been essential to its success. Knowing that the Cadre needed to move to "the next level," in this case to the university setting, and finding a university professor to take on the project, also helped keep the Waldorf-inspired Cadre alive and vibrant.

Planning. A strong leader recognizes the importance of careful and inspired planning. Inherent in this planning is a shared decision-making process. Before setting the agenda of the Cadre's academic year, Caroline and I always sit down with Cadre members and plan the year's events, based on the collective needs of the members. According to Wood et al. (1989), professional development must be based on clear, specific objectives, congruent with goals selected by teachers. Careful planning also includes strong communication. As previously mentioned, all correspondence to Cadre members and friends goes out on e-mail and then again through U.S. mail, followed by a second and sometimes third e-mail announcement. Instructors and presenters for workshops and classes are contacted at least six months in advance, and conversations take place in plenty of time to plan each upcoming event. Robinson and Darling-Hammond (2005) concur. "Establishing efficient means for members of the collaboration to communicate within and across institutional boundaries is essential to success" (p. 216).

Fiscal Support. Financial support is paramount in the ongoing success of our program. Subsequently, critical in the initial phases was the collaboration and support from Janey Newton and her Creative Education Foundation. Without continued funding from the Norton Foundation, I truly doubt that this project would still be in operation. I have worked with professional-development projects in other states and districts, and when the funding dries up, it is extremely difficult to keep things going. Most people cannot afford to work for free, even if the effort is in the best interests of everyone involved. Robinson and Darling Hammond (2005) believe that outside funding legitimizes projects and helps those involved take risks and break free from the status quo. I wholeheartedly agree.

Administrative Support. Throughout the tenure of the Cadre, administrative support at all levels has been instrumental. JCPS administrators, including building principals as well as upper-level leadership, offer support in numerous ways. Principals attend workshops and try to learn more about Waldorf-inspired methods. Furthermore, I have been hired by principals to offer professional development in Waldorf-inspired practices for their teachers. Some principals support their Cadre teachers financially by paying for their training. In recent years, principals who support this type of whole-child learning in the midst of enormous pressures "to improve test scores" have shown a deep belief that their Cadre teachers are implementing the curriculum with methodology supported through current educational research. Furthermore, Cadre members can articulate and demonstrate that Waldorf-inspired methods meet district and state curriculum mandates. In addition to public-school administrative support, I receive support at the university level. From additional funding to the approval of such a unique graduate program, the university leadership provides this informal recognition. Wood et al. (1989), contend that even with adequate help to implement professional development, lasting change is unlikely to occur without the support of the principal and other administrators.

Training and Maintenance. As evidenced by the detailed accounts in this chapter, training for teachers has been ongoing since the inception of the project. In addition, research on effective training shows that programs must be dynamic, engaging, and experiential. Although I am extremely close to this project, I know that workshops and trainings contain each of the above three elements. This is evidenced by the feedback from participants. Furthermore, maintenance of the program is a large part of my work. Mentoring teachers and continuous review, along with timely communications and, as previously mentioned, a very hands-on approach, all help maintain the project.

Ongoing Commitment. Thus far, commitment from all parties involved in the project has been strong. From continuous funding to enthused and active teachers, the Waldorf-inspired Cadre is alive and well. This does not mean that all Cadre members stay one-hundred percent involved throughout their teaching careers. Many teachers in the Cadre have come and gone. However, there remains a strong core of committed individuals who bring a depth and breadth to the project, helping to maintain and legitimize the incredible work of all teachers involved.

Reflection and Evaluation. Inherent in all good teaching and learning is reflection. Reflecting at the end of a school day or week helps teachers evaluate and make sense of their practice. Reflecting on the success of a mentoring session or a workshop or a two-week institute is critical to the success of this program. Ongoing evaluation is also a key ingredient. Each year when I write the grant proposal, I am required to reflect on and evaluate the previous year's work. This evaluation process is invaluable to me as director of the project, as I can take a more global view of the work and make decisions about what was successful and what was not. Long-term evaluation and reflection is also critical in the legitimization of a project such as this. By completing this research project on the Waldorf-inspired Cadre, all involved feel that their work is valued and respected.

These aspects constitute the known and common ingredients for a strong and successful professional development program. However, many projects with these key factors have come and gone throughout the history of staff development. What makes the ongoing success of this project unique is the uncommon element—that of meeting the teachers' soul needs. Sam Intrator and Robert Kunzman, both students of Parker Palmer, believe that "the way to truly increase teachers' capacities is to engage their souls" (2006, 39). They go on to discuss organizational-research findings that contend "collective passion and mission" (p. 39) as the essential core for enduring success. The Waldorf-inspired Cadre Project imbues these qualities. Not only do teachers share a passion for bringing Waldorf-inspired methods to their students, they instinctively know the importance of nurturing their spirits. Waldorf-inspired practices rekindle the energy and passion needed to sustain strong, inspired teaching, both long and short term.

The following chapters illustrate more deeply the value of teachers' work with their students. Chapter three looks at the way in which a Waldorf-inspired pedagogy helps to build community in the classroom, whereas the fourth chapter speaks to the engaging methods teachers implement. The fifth chapter more thoroughly explores the way in which Waldorf education helps to deepen the teacher's inner life.

3

BUILDING COMMUNITY

"Teaching at its best, is an enterprise that helps human beings reach the full measure of their humanity... it embraces as principle and overarching purpose the aspiration of people to become more fully human; it impels us toward further knowledge, enlightenment, and human community—toward liberation." (William Ayers 2004, 1)

IN OUR FAST-PACED, FRAGMENTED WORLD, the need for community is stronger than ever before. In David Korten's (2006) intriguing book, *The Great Turning: From Earth Empire to Community,* he discusses the fact that the human race has had hundreds of thousands of years of living in community and only five-thousand years of empire building. Yet the building of the empires has led to a society fraught with violence and individualism. Parker Palmer (1999) writes about the secular nature of education, complete with its distance, coldness, and a lack of community, but goes on to say that this is just the view on the surface. If one goes deep "to the depths you go when you seek that which is sacred, you find the hidden wholeness. You find the community that a good teacher evokes and invites students into, that weaves and reweaves our lives, alone and together" (p. 27). During the height of the school-reform movement, community building, especially in the middle school, became a part of the school day. However, with the implementation of No Child Left Behind (NCLB), exactly the opposite has occurred, and many children have been left further behind than before the demoralizing law went into effect. Nel Noddings, noted educator on caring and schools concurs: "Surely, we should demand more from our schools than to educate people to be proficient in reading and mathematics" (2006, 10). Even when schools have attempted to include community building in their already overloaded curriculum, it has been a rather fragmented attempt, seen as a separate class, wherein benign posters with words such as *kindness* and *cooperation* grace the walls.

Noddings (2006) believes that working within our subject-centered curriculum, teachers can still address social, moral, emotional and aesthetic issues. Steiner (2003) referred to this as "soul economy." One of the beauties of the Waldorf curriculum is just that: Steiner's soul economy ensures that every subject is deeply integrated with the issues mentioned, as well as with a reverence and respect for self, one another, and the planet. The whole Waldorf school day is intended to facilitate a strong classroom community. The methods Waldorf schools use to build community are certainly one aspect that Cadre members have taken into their public-school classrooms.

Through the many interviews and classroom observations with Cadre members, I found community building to be a common theme in their classrooms. Within the larger context of community, which Mathew Fox (2006) defines as something natural to ourselves and to the rest of nature, I found there to be two sub-themes: a republic of many voices and a controlled freedom. Included in each of the two sub-themes is a number of smaller categories, each of which will be described in detail.

A REPUBLIC OF MANY VOICES

William Ayers (2004) believes that teachers must make a commitment to create a space in their classrooms where "a republic of many voices might come to life, the 'uniculture' opposed, and the suffocating sameness of the domineering voice resisted" (p. 69). He goes on to say that teachers must "build an environment where human beings can face one another authentically and without masks, a place of invitation, fascination, interest, and promise. The focus here is on the environment for learning; the physical space, of course, and, perhaps more important, the spiritual and ethical and intellectual and social spaces that only a teacher can ignite" (p. 69). I found this "republic of many voices" apparent in nearly all of the Cadre teachers' classrooms. These inclusive classrooms built community by teaching students to accept one another's differences, building confidence, creating self-directed learners, allowing the healthy emergence of leaders, and assisting teachers in getting to know their students in a deeper, more authentic way.

Getting to Know the Students

One way teachers in the Cadre regularly created the opportunity to build community and get to know their students better was through the use of the "morning circle," a common feature found in Waldorf schools the world over. Before starting the circle, teachers begin their day by greeting students individually at the door, creating a ritual that Richards (1980) describes as "a moment's pause at the doorway, a contact, a greeting, an affirmation of identity and affectionate respect: an acknowledgment of meaningful time spent together" (p. 51). Debbie Lockyear, former kindergarten teacher at Hartstern Elementary, spoke about her incorporation of greeting the children at the beginning of the day and how it helped create a bond between herself and her students.

> It showed me that [greeting] just gives them a sense of comfort…maybe it seals the bond between the adult and the student so when they're feeling upset or if they're worried they did something and got into trouble, they were able to come and talk to me or they were more loving. (personal interview)

Debbie went on to say that, at the beginning of the school year, she was the only teacher who greeted her students at the door, and as the year progressed, other teachers began to do this as well.

After teachers greet their children, the circle follows, which is an intentional academic-group activity where students learn content through songs, poems, movement, and games. A typical circle for a fourth-grade class may last anywhere from ten to twenty minutes. Students gather in an actual circle and as witnessed in Patty Rundell's class, a former fourth- and fifth-grade teacher at Lowe Elementary, students began with the poem "Brave and True," followed by another poem by Christina Rossetti, "Hurt No Living Thing." After poetry, the students sang songs about the brain, growing plants, and ended with a round, "Music Alone Shall Live." Following the songs, Patty passed out beanbags to all the students. The dissemination of the beanbags took place while students sang a rhythmic song. Students then did a movement activity with the bean bags and ended the circle with another poem.

According to Kris Raitzer, principal at Lowe, Patty asked Kris to come in and watch her class circle at the beginning of the 2003 school year. Patty had a tough crew of fifth graders, yet she went in with the mindset that each kid would be successful and was determined that they were going to work as a community. Kris went to Patty's classroom during the first week of school and stayed about forty minutes.

> Even in that first week, she had built a sense of community and a sense of caring and calm and peace in her classroom unlike other classrooms that I have seen.... Within that first week, that was established as part of the culture of the classroom— that peacefulness and sort of kindness. And I could see that strand ran throughout the school year in her classroom. It was just always a little bit quieter place, probably a happier place to be, a place where kids really wanted to be, and a place where kids really talked about their ideas and opinions and connections more than other classrooms. (personal interview)

Other teachers, too, spoke of the way in which the circle grounds the kids and prepares them for the day. Patty Gilderbloom, former fifth-grade teacher at Byck Elementary, states:

We do a circle in the morning [which] incorporates a lot of the core content skills through that circle [Kentucky requires a core content that all teachers must teach], as well, but it's a community-builder. It is a time for the kids to come together and try to start the day off on the right footing. It's a wonderful time, actually, especially in the public schools where everything is very high-stress, and everything goes so quickly. It is a time for us to gather our thoughts at the beginning of the day and prepare ourselves for a hectic day. (personal interview)

Donna Stottman, former fifth-grade teacher at Blue Lick Elementary also remarked that the morning helped build community in her classroom and helped her assess the children's mood in the morning.

Community is important, which was something that I didn't count on when I first decided to do this [Waldorf-inspired education]. I did not realize it would fit so well with building community.... When we all start circle in the morning, not only can we see where they're at, but also what kind of day they might have, how their focus is that day, and whether it will be a good day. They get to do something together as a whole group. Each individual part matters, and when we are all together we can do such beautiful things. (personal interview)

Patty Gilderbloom concurred. She spoke of the circle as a way to get to know the children.

It's also a way to get to know each child, as well as his or her strengths and weaknesses, and to let their strengths grow and shine. So there are many aspects of Waldorf education that really help both the teacher get to know the students better, and the students get to know themselves and each other better in the meantime. (personal interview)

Self-directed Learners and the Creation of Healthy Leaders

One of the greatest gifts we can give to our students is that of becoming self-directed learners. This type of self-direction is not narcissistic, rather it is a discipline that allows students to discover who they are as learners so that they can take charge of their learning and get the most of their education. Students who are self-directed tend to be more creative, satisfied, and often emerge as leaders. In a Waldorf-inspired setting, teachers encourage the development of the whole child, so that students develop emotionally, mentally, and physically. When teachers create a community of learners, when everyone has a voice, students are allowed to be themselves, to become more of who they really are.

When I asked Shannon Conlon, former principal at Byck Elementary, about the community aspect of the Cadre teachers' classrooms, she said:

> I see more of the whole child being educated in these classrooms. They really not only talk about respect and community, they walk the talk. I see kids taking ownership and buying in, that they have this community. I would say that's the biggest—watching them do the circle and infusing the arts.... They have this ownership in their education.... I don't see it as a rule driven place.... I see it as a community. They do have some rules, but they're few. And the students help decide what they are and how to make it more of their community. It's very student-centered, not teacher-centered. I think it sets the tone of how they interact with adults, their peers within the classroom and outside the classroom. I think it trickles over into classrooms that aren't [inspired by] Waldorf education. (personal interview)

Students' ownership in the classroom helps spawn self-directed young people. Their teachers, according to Bill Ayers (2004) "stand on the side of [the] students. We [teachers] create a space where their [students'] voices can be heard, their experiences affirmed, their lives valued, their humanity asserted, enacted" (p. 102). By creating this space, students are able to be more self-directed and assume more leadership roles, something we desperately want our students to imbue. Patty Gilderbloom talked about the transference of power in her classroom and how that helped her students take more ownership of their education.

> [Teaching] becomes a combined effort...kids behave when they have to behave...children...engage in their own teaching, so to speak, or they take ownership of their education.... To me, that's the only way kids will really learn anything—if they take control and take charge of it. After the Commonwealth Achievement Test, we do three major projects that have a lot of Waldorf-inspired methods to go along with them.... In these projects, kids take ownership of their own education. (personal interview)

Patty also noticed a difference in the children who had received a Waldorf-inspired education for all of their schooling (as previously mentioned, Byck has a team of teachers, grades K–5, who use Waldorf-inspired methods in their classrooms and the students stay with this same cohort as they progress through the grades), as opposed to those students who just joined her classroom as fifth-graders.

> I see a real difference between the children who have had the Waldorf-inspired training in a sense from kindergarten on...and I had a lot of those children last year, and there is a real difference in the self-discipline, the self-motivation.... This past year, I had a lot of students who were experiencing Waldorf-inspired methods for the first time. It was really quite glaring, the differences. But as soon as the kids understood what was expected of them, they followed suit and really followed along with the other children who'd had the methodology presented to them since maybe first- or second-grade or even kindergarten. (personal interview)

Patty continued by discussing the quality of the work and the increased problem-solving skills that the students began to take up.

> Once the kids caught on to what was expected of them, they really did strive for quality and learned not to always ask

questions; learned to think things through by themselves; and looked for the answers within rather than quickly raising their hands to get an answer. They learned how to do problem-solving by themselves. And I think that's the beauty of Waldorf education—the kids are taught to think and not to have a quick answer all of the time, which so many of the children want to do these days. You know, it is a consumable world and they want an easy answer right away. (personal interview)

Debbie Lockyear also saw her kindergarten students display more patience and quality when doing Waldorf-inspired work. During a guided-drawing lesson, a technique practiced in Waldorf schools to help children learn to draw through form, Debbie noted:

I think with the guided drawing, it helped them learn some patience, learn some listening techniques.... Little kindergartners want to wiggle and squirm, and do what they want all of the time. And my assistant was always amazed that, during that time [of guided drawing], they were so good at listening, being still, and following directions. And it was amazing, too, to see the product of their guided drawings.... When they take time they really get a sense of what is going on and are able to complete the picture. (personal interview)

Because Waldorf education stresses the importance of developmentally appropriate pedagogy, Patty's and Debbie's students benefited from a number of aspects of this approach. First, by delving more deeply into the subject matter, not just skimming the surface, students are allowed to immerse themselves in something—a real luxury in today's culture. Second, the expectation of quality, another hallmark of Waldorf education, is something missing from most educational settings today. Spending more time on a project, doing one's best work, making something beautiful—all of this has become a lost art. Children today are pushed to "learn" more at an earlier and earlier age, to become *academically* (note the absence of *socially* and *emotionally*) proficient by a specific time, whereas all this really does is distance students from the pure love of learning. Furthermore, by allowing children to learn through the arts, they are awakened in a truly heartfelt way that connects them to whatever they are learning. The intention of creating students who love learning for its own sake and building their confidence through this love, is another tenant of Waldorf education. Patty reiterated this:

> The kids that were taught this kind of methodology [Waldorf] really do allow themselves more—they dig deeper into their souls and their minds about trying to get answers from within rather than from without or from somebody else. They rely more on themselves and they have greater confidence. I think it's because they have been able to express themselves through so many mediums, and have had success expressing themselves that way. I think their whole outlook on themselves and how they relate to the world is very different. (personal interview)

In addition to building confidence and helping kids become more self-sufficient in their learning, pedagogy inspired by Waldorf education has also helped children grow socially and emotionally, and in so doing, they accept one another's differences.

Accepting Differences

Parker Palmer (1999) believes that "if we could recover a sense of the sacred in knowing, teaching, and learning, we could recover our sense of the *otherness* of the things in our world" (p. 23). Palmer goes on to say that reductionism in education happens when we try and cram everything we study into categories, ignoring the things that don't fit into our reality. Fearing otherness "flattens our intellectual terrain" (p. 24) and takes away the richness, the beauty, and the sacredness of what the other may have to offer us. Moore (1996) discusses teaching similarity and differences in the multicultural approach to education as an opportunity for creating growth through connection (seeing what we have in common) and through challenge (using our differences as a chance for new possibilities). By integrating Waldorf-inspired pedagogy, Cadre teachers have seamlessly woven this respect for difference and for the "other" through their modeling and through the messages inherent in the multidimensional methodologies.

When Donna Stottman was team-teaching with Tina Marstellar at Blue Lick Elementary, they named their classes the sun group and the moon group, rather than calling them Ms. Stottman's and Ms. Marstellar's classes. They believed this took away the temptation to point out differences between the two groups. According to Donna "it's just much kinder this way" (personal interview). Donna discussed their morning circle and how it helped the children accept one another's differences:

> The movement [in the circle] has helped my kids. They have a better connection with one another. That is one way they are the same, because even if they're different academically or with behavior, everyone drops a beanbag, not everyone can sing, people miss lines in the verses we say. We do the verse "Welcome to Success" [see next page], and I think about that with my kids. You *will* be successful in here. You will be. It will happen for you. (personal interview)

After teaching at Blue Lick, Tina transferred to Lowe Elementary, where she began teaching with two other Cadre members (Patty Rundell and Jennifer Geroski). Principal Kris Raitzer, spoke about Tina:

> Tina came a couple of years ago. And so my third-, fourth-, and fifth-grade classrooms are all Waldorf-inspired. Again, when I walk into Tina's classroom, I see kids who understand the idea of community and of learning together and accepting each other's differences, being understanding of each other's differences. (personal interview)

Another Cadre teacher, Mona Jones, spoke about circle as a way to build social skills in her classroom. As mentioned, children recite poetry and work on speech exercises (among other things) in the morning circle. Mona had the opportunity for a group of superintendents to observe her class, and one was so impressed with the children that he wrote her a letter. She shared some of that letter: "He wrote about how

WELCOME TO SUCCESS

Welcome to success
A place where we do our best
We respect, encourage, and support one another
We never laugh at, put down, or discourage another
We may be children but we have great dreams
Working together, we can achieve anything
Welcome to success
A place where we do our best

powerful it is to teach children how to speak and act in front of people, because he said you can be a really smart kid and yet be unable to keep a job without social skills" (personal interview). Mona also talked about how the circle encourages cooperation in her classroom. The children in her class value the morning circle and the artistic activities she brings to them so much that they self-correct their behavior and work at getting along with one another, because they don't want to miss the opportunity to join the group in the circle activities.

Debbie Lockyear also commented on circle time as helping her young students "gel" as a class. She felt as if, during circle time, her students learned many relational aspects of community and actually became more of a family.

Kris Raitzer mentioned in our interview that the Cadre members' students are different in their social and emotional growth. They are kinder to one another; they support and respect one another's differences. Parker Palmer describes good teachers as people who have the capacity to connect themselves and their students to one another and to the subject studied. "I have become increasingly convinced that this recovery of community is at the heart of good teaching" (Palmer 1999, 27).

In addition to the aspects of community-building mentioned, Cadre members also build community through what one member calls "controlled freedom," which is found throughout their teaching. From the use of creative transitions to the integration of artistic activities and to the well-loved morning circle, Cadre teachers have found ways to implement Waldorf-inspired education into the state-mandated core content. Although Patty Gilderbloom talked about this controlled freedom in terms of her students' behavior, I also see the teachers exercising their freedom in the classroom—a risky undertaking in the current public-school climate. By taking the initiative to teach in this way, teachers have not allowed themselves to be disempowered by the status quo, which, according to Thomas Armstrong (2006), also disempowers students.

CONTROLLED FREEDOM

In the introduction of Bill Ayers's (2004) stunning book, *Teaching toward Freedom: Moral Commitment and Ethical Action in the Classroom,* he writes: "Each morning, as we rise and venture toward a new day, and later, as we approach our classrooms, we might remind ourselves that a teacher's destination is always the same: that special spot between heaven and earth, that plain but spectacular space where we might once again try to teach toward freedom" (xv). I saw Cadre teachers striving toward this freedom as they tirelessly brought teaching inspired by Waldorf education to their students on a regular basis. This section further explores the building of community through ritual, respect, and how Waldorf-inspired teaching helps students make good choices.

Ritual

According to Mathew Fox (2006), "There is no community without ceremony and ritual" (p. 136). He says that community means sharing joys and sorrows, building strength together, and having the courage to carry on. He also believes that rituals and ceremonies recharge us, heal us, and energize us. Rituals also allow students to feel safe and held and teach a kind of reverence and respect that technical teaching cannot. Rituals build community by helping children instill a deeper meaning into their feeling life. Donna Stottman talked at length about the ritual nature of the morning handshake and circle.

It's real important that they have something constant, something consistent to count on. The ritual of it—they can count on that. We're going to do that every day no matter what. It is sacred. They know what's going on.... It's funny, too, with organization [of the circle] they start to know the order and it's real ritual for awhile, and then you're ready to change, so you drop something and they ask, "What happened to [the song] 'Dockside Cries'? We did not do it!" (personal interview)

Although ritual is present in nearly every classroom, public and private, the nature of ritual in a Waldorf school or in a Cadre member's classroom is somehow different. It's more respectful and reverent, owing to the content of the ritual. Donna team-taught with Brenda Chelliah for two years at Blue Lick: "I always tried to do cooperative games, and we would do the games, play them a few times, and then be done. But circle is every day. That is how I think it's different" (personal interview). Brenda echoed Donna's thoughts: "I always did community-building stuff. It would be sprinkled into some lesson or new game that we would try. But the circle is different. The songs and poems and movements have a different quality—more heartfelt" (personal interview). The heartfelt nature of the circle, along with the aspect of ritual, was also apparent in the transitions Cadre teachers used in their classrooms.

Respectful Transitions

Bruce Urmacher (1991) wrote that Waldorf schools introduce elements of reverence and respect into their teaching by using symbols, rituals, and ceremonies, and that teachers use their daily curriculum to introduce these elements as well. According to Henry Barnes (1999), noted Waldorf educator and author, "Waldorf education, in a conscious and intended way, provides the child with opportunities all through the grades to develop an attitude of respect and wonder toward the world. These are an intrinsic part of the Waldorf curriculum" (p. 5). One way to weave respect into the school day is through transitions. All successful teachers know the value of a good transition. They are points in the school day when the teacher can either lose valuable teaching time or smoothly move from one subject or topic into the next. I found that Cadre teachers use transitions not only to move the children seamlessly into the next activity, but also to take advantage of that time in a very intentional, respectful way to teach their students content.

While observing Brad Nance, a kindergarten teacher at Byck Elementary, I was delighted (as were his students) with a fun transition song that taught short and long vowel sounds. After his children finished with a story, he began this song:

> I like to eat, I like to eat, I like to eat apples and bananas, I like to ITE I like to ITE, I like to ITE IPPLES and BININAS. EE like to EAT, EE like to EAT, EE like to EAT EEPLES and BEENEENEES.

His students all joined in singing the song as they moved without incident to the carpet. There they began their next activity and worked on short- and long-vowel sounds in a fun, engaging manner. Donna talked about transitions as a way to treat her children with greater respect:

> I was just thinking about how I love not yelling at the kids. I'm hooked on chimes [Donna uses chimes to get her students' attention]. The transitions are so much smoother, and you don't even have to think about it.... I just keep thinking about the transitions, because I see so many teachers in the hallway and in other classrooms so harsh ... and if my students are having a bad moment or I cannot get them focused, I just whip out a verse or I can start singing a song ... and it takes five seconds ... it is just so much better than yelling "Hey!" (personal interview)

Private Waldorf school teachers routinely sing transitions to their children in the primary grades, whereas they use other methods for the older children. I find it interesting that the intermediate-grade Cadre teachers use singing effectively for their transitions. Perhaps this is because many public-school children do not experience school as a pleasant, respectful place, and singing is more peaceful and engaging than other methods used to get their attention.

In addition to these kinds of transitions, Cadre teachers also found that many other aspects of the Waldorf curriculum and pedagogy encouraged positive behavior in their students.

Instilling Positive Behavior

Thomas Armstrong (2006) believes that, when education focuses on academic achievement, students who cannot achieve are much more likely to misbehave in the classroom. He states:

> When students are engaged in classroom activities that engage their social, emotional, creative, physical, and spiritual selves, they are far less likely to *need* to engage in activities designed to subvert the learning process. (p. 63)

According to Rachel Naomi Ramen (1999), "Educators are healers. Educators and healers both trust in the wholeness of life and in the wholeness of people.... We must have the courage to educate people to heal this world into what it might become" (p. 35). Throughout my interviews and observations of Cadre members' classrooms, I saw this philosophy in action. Cadre teachers engaged their students in ways that reduced and, in many cases, eliminated behavior problems; they held fast to the belief that their children are whole, spiritual human beings, capable of great things and deserving real respect.

Debbie Lockyear and Kelly Cole talked about other teachers who noticed how well-behaved and engaged their children were. Kelly shared this story:

> A really good teacher whom I respect a lot asked, "What is it that you were doing with them outside?" (We do it [the circle] outside when it's nice.) "They were so attentive and they were really into it. What is it? You'll have to tell me about that."... [Hearing] an outsider's perspective, made me feel like "Oh yeah, it *is* what I think it is. It is as good as I think." (personal interview)

Debbie also received positive feedback from her assistant, who, at the beginning of the school year, had been unfamiliar with the Waldorf-inspired methods Debbie used in her classroom:

> My assistant... was always amazed. And one of her quotes all of the time was, "Always, always they're being so wonderful during your Waldorf activity. Why don't they do this the rest of the day?" (personal interview)

As we can see, Cadre teachers do not replicate the Waldorf day, nor can they use the Waldorf curriculum. Kentucky, as mentioned, has a mandated core content. Cadre teachers are nonetheless creative in their approaches to teaching that core content; the Waldorf-inspired methods they use continuously help student behavior.

Occupational and physical therapists in the district also began asking questions such as, "What are you doing in the classroom? There is such an improvement." According to Caroline, those therapists saw differences in the children who had been knitting and weaving in their classrooms.

Parents also noticed the difference in student behavior. Caroline shared this story:

> As they [teachers] implemented elements of Waldorf, parents saw a change.... Parents were coming and commenting on this, particularly with kids who had behavior problems. And one kid in particular (I'm thinking of a student whose teacher said he was very volatile) would burst out, would break things, throw things. The parent was at the end of her rope dealing with this child. [The child] would punch holes in the wall. He had ruined a TV because he had kicked it. Well, he took up knitting, loved it. And I think the real telling part of it is when his parents came and told the teacher, "You know what he did? He got so mad, I was afraid he was going to break things. And he said, 'Well, I think I'll just go knit.' And he went to his room and knitted." I thought, "My goodness, what an avenue for those kids who are having problems and need something to do with their hands to help calm them down." (personal interview)

Caroline related another story about a child who had neurological problems and was struggling socially and academically. His teacher, Dan Torpey, a member of the Cadre, started weaving and knitting with his students. The child took to the knitting and weaving, which calmed him. He became very good at weaving and knitting, which leveled the playing field, as the more academically talented students struggled in this area. Caroline related:

> The change that came about in this student and his relationship to his peers was another positive aspect. So if you look at the student work, the improvement in student work, particularly in behavior, you can see the positive results of Waldorf-inspired methods. (personal interview)

Another group of high-school teachers decided to join the Cadre and incorporate Waldorf-inspired methods into their teaching. These teachers were working with high-school students who were not eligible for special-education services and were on the verge of dropping out of school. Some were involved in the court system and were in a program that allowed them to continue their schooling. The teachers set up a unique, theme-based program in which they integrated movement, dance, music, drama, and painting into their English, mathematics, and social studies. Performance days were then organized so students could share what they had accomplished with one another and with parents. According to Caroline, the teachers began to see an improvement in attendance. She shared the following story.

> There was a student who was struggling terribly in school, and she came up to her teachers and said (for the first time really interacted in a positive way with them instead of calling them names that we won't repeat here), "Oh, please do me a favor. I have a court date on the day that we have our performance. Can we change the date?" Well, they changed the date for her, and the other kids saw that the teachers were really trying to work with them. From that incident more kids attended, and on performance day they had one-hundred-percent participation.

Now, for those kids who would lose their way going to school, who were on the verge of dropping out, this kept kids in school. In fact, one English teacher taught AP [advanced placement] English classes in the morning and this special group in the afternoon. Kids in her AP English class were complaining, because they were not getting to paint, they were not getting to do movement.... I think when you look at the change in kids, the parents notice it, teachers notice it. They cannot put their finger on it, but I think these elements of Waldorf education have a deep and long-lasting meaning. (personal interview)

The high-school Cadre teachers were not the only ones who noticed a difference with their "fringe" students. Donna discussed the impact that her Waldorf-inspired teaching had on one of her students.

One of my kids was angry, angry, angry all the time last year. He's a really *move-ey* kid—very distractible.... The art teacher saw that he was on my class list...and she said "Oh, are you ready for this?" And I'm like, don't tell me. I don't want to know anything about him. I just want to meet him myself. And the second time we went to art, which is every three weeks for a week, she said, "He is so different. He is so happy." (personal interview)

Brenda taught with Donna at one time, and she, too, commented on this art teacher:

She's very observant, our art teacher, very tuned-in with where our kids are behaviorally, and she said the same thing about one of my students. She said "Oh wow, he's doing so great this year. Last year, he was on point sheets every day.... Behaviorally, he's doing much better." (personal interview)

Brenda spoke about a violent child who was in her special-education classroom. He would even throw desks, but when it was time for the morning circle, he would do anything to participate. It became a way to reach out to this child.

All of my research points to the fact that Waldorf-inspired pedagogy helps all kinds of children. Whether a student is of elementary age or in high school, struggles academically or is gifted, has a label of some sort or another—methods inspired by Waldorf education benefit all kids.

CONCLUSION

In a 1999 lecture by bell hooks at the Naropa Institute, she was asked this question: "What are we doing as educators to bring a spirit of compassion, of interbeing, into our classrooms?"(p. 121). Along with countless educators, hooks understands the importance of infusing our educational system with a sense of community, compassion, and caring. Rachel Naomi Ramen (1999) echoes these thoughts:

> Of all the contemporary cultural institutions, education holds the greatest promise for healing the wounds of the cultural shadow. In some ways, education has historically held this responsibility. *Educare,* the root of the word *education,* means "to lead forth the hidden wholeness," the innate integrity that is in every person. (p. 35)

I am convinced that Waldorf-inspired education has the capacity to heal. Members of the Cadre echo my sentiments. Education inspired by Waldorf methodology has helped teachers across our school district build community in their classrooms—community that is deep and meaningful. They know their students intimately and have allowed their classrooms to be safe places, where everyone has a voice and where all voices are respected equally. Teachers trust their students to take charge of their own behavior in a way that honors each individual's freedom. As James Comer (1998) states so eloquently, "We weren't taught values; we caught values in an environment in which desirable values were acted out all the time" (p. 7).

Waldorf-inspired education has enhanced student behavior as well as the teachers' respect and reverence for the children in their care. It is a way of teaching that wraps its arms around everyone present, embracing the good and allowing the emergence of true community.

Teachers sense a renewed awe and wonder for the communities created in their classrooms. They have also shared the impact of Waldorf-inspired methods on their students' engagement in academic subjects.

4

ENGAGING STUDENTS

*"Our task is to find teaching methods that continually
engage the whole human being." (Rudolf Steiner 2000, 5)*

RUDOLF STEINER SPOKE THESE WORDS in 1919 to the future teachers
of the first Waldorf school in Stuttgart, Germany. His message
remains critically significant for teachers in the twenty-first century.
As discussed in the previous chapter, children crave meaning in their
lives. One way to give meaning is through a strong classroom community. Cadre teachers have discovered that their students also gain
meaning through a deep engagement in their Waldorf-inspired methods. Rachel Kessler (2000) believes that when teachers bring opportunities for students to find and create meaning—to engage wholeheartedly in their education—they contribute substantially to the
students' spiritual development. Noted author of *Raising Boys*, Steve
Biddulph (1997), states, "Boys and girls crave an engaged and intense
learning experience with men and women who challenge them and get
to know them personally—and from this specific knowledge of their
needs, work with them to shape and extend their intellect, spirit, and
skills" (p. 130).

This chapter considers the many ways that teachers and students
explore the landscape of learning. From my time spent in teachers'

classrooms, as well as through interviews, it became clear that Cadre teachers consistently went beyond "best practice" as currently conceived, and that this way of interacting with their students resulted in excitement and a true love for education.

BEYOND BEST PRACTICE

Zemelman, Daniels, and Hyde (1998) identify "best practices" with these key principles and theories: child-centered, experiential, reflective, authentic, holistic, social, collaborative, democratic, cognitive, developmental, constructivist, psycholinguistic, and challenging. Since the publication of their first book on best practices in 1993, the term has come to roll a bit too easily off the tongues of administrators and teachers across the country. Given the rather lengthy list of key principles, it is not difficult to see how best practices might have become coopted. When I hear the term bantered about today, I pay little attention or question what the "banterer" actually means. Perhaps I have become a bit spoiled by my association with Waldorf education. I consider the teaching in a Waldorf school and by teachers in the Cadre to be education that goes beyond best practices. Each of the thirteen key theories mentioned wend their way throughout a Cadre teacher's classroom, but in a deeply integrated, respectful, and reverent way.

Borrowing from the highly engaged teaching in private Waldorf schools, Cadre members successfully integrate a number of methods inspired by Waldorf education into their classrooms. For example, teachers use storytelling as a vehicle to teach mathematics, social studies, and science. Given that a significant amount of curriculum geared for elementary students is developmentally inappropriate, storytelling is used to create images for children, which helps them understand the concepts in ways that meet their particular stage of development. "Storytelling appeals to children's imaginations and emotions and helps make learning more meaningful. When children listen to stories, they create mental images that belong to them, connecting the content to something personally significant" (Goral and Gnadinger 2006, 4).

A Waldorf-inspired main-lesson book

Storytelling engages children's feeling life, which helps them connect to and sustain content.

Cadre members, as mentioned, also integrate Gardner's (1983) multiple intelligences, but in a way that honors the content. In other words, intelligence is not the main focus; rather, the intention is to bring the content to the children in a myriad of ways to further their understanding. Teachers use movement, song, and poetry extensively in the morning circle. Art is woven into the core content throughout the day. Students create main-lesson books, using colored pencils and beeswax crayons, just as children do in private Waldorf schools. Wet-on-wet painting delights students of all ages. Children paint images from the curriculum, which not only engages their feeling life, but helps to sustain their memory of particular concepts. Cadre teachers teach their students to knit, and as recounted in chapter three, this assists students' fine motor skill development, aids some children with neurological problems, and helps calm students. Although teachers are not able to use Waldorf-inspired methods the entire day, the times that they do integrate the pedagogy helps engage and inspire children.

Using the Arts to Enhance Teaching

The fine arts, such as painting and drawing, are perhaps the most used artistic mediums in Cadre members' classrooms. Although Jan Kovac is an art teacher, she commented that she's able to use many Waldorf-inspired methods and that she "uses the arts to teach art." While visiting Jan's classroom at Jeffersontown Elementary, I saw the following:

> Jan started the class with a song. "Heads down all around, every head is down." Children became quiet immediately. The class then locked arms and Jan spoke in soft voice. She sang the attendance, just as teachers in a private Waldorf school do. Children then sang "The Rainbow Song." The kids stood up and pushed in their chairs and sang "Red, orange, yellow, green, and blue" to the tune of "Heads, Shoulders, Knees, and Toes." Because Jan has to teach elements of design to young children, she made up a song with movements to the words "Vertical, horizontal, diagonal, spiral, free form—wild and wiggle, and dot and sit on the spot." After the song, children sat down and Jan recited another short poem to have the first-graders put their hands in their laps. "Open them close them, open them close them, give them a little clap. Open them close them, open them close them, put them in your lap." She then introduced a line-design assignment by telling the children a story about pioneers and quilt-making. (from field notes)

During my interview with Jan, she elaborated on what I had seen in her classroom.

> I do a rainbow song, the line-design movement, and then I will do a direction dance/movement—kind of rhythmic thing that has to do with vertical, horizontal, diagonal, spiral, and radial direction.... The children lead this. They love it, I mean all the way down to kindergarten, they know vertical, horizontal, diagonal, spiral, and almost within the first couple of weeks. Before I started using movement and song to teach these concepts (which

are difficult for young children to remember), it had to be done in a short period of time and it was almost beyond my reach. We also create, I call them master-plan books, main-lesson books. (personal interview)

Because Jan is an art teacher she can use the arts to teach art, whereas other Cadre teachers integrate the arts into their academic subject areas.

Mona Jones, long-time Cadre member, talked about the fact that her extensive experience with Waldorf education has helped her integrate the arts into much of her curriculum.

They make borders in their main-lesson books, they write about the content, and they paint it, too.... But I think the reason that I really use it [Waldorf-inspired pedagogy] continually and feel very good about it is that children learn better that way. They learn the core content. And I have to teach the core content, and that's fine. But, when they draw it and write about it and use colored pencils to write about it and use beeswax crayons, they are able to really remember and be engaged in what I'm teaching. (personal interview)

Debbie Lockyear integrated watercolor painting into her science lessons.

Whenever we would do a science lesson, we would incorporate a Waldorf-style painting. We worked on creating our key animals, a snake and a fish, when we talked about blending the colors and things like that. And so we did about four paintings this year... and they were amazing. (personal interview)

Fifth-graders in Donna and Tina's class also painted to enhance the learning of science concepts. While studying plants, Donna and Tina had their students create a series of pumpkin paintings. I had the privilege of witnessing the third painting in the series.

When I entered Donna's room, she had three steps written on the board to help students begin the creation of their pumpkin paintings. The words *Gold, Gold, Yellow,* and *Orange, Gold,* and

Yellow, were written in colored chalk in three separate boxes.
Donna used language such as realism and shadow, and had several real pumpkins in the room for children to observe. Donna spoke in a quiet voice.... Students were relatively quiet and the collecting of supplies [painting boards, paper, sponges, rags and brushes] went smoothly. Students then began the lesson with a painting verse. "I look into the sky where the sun shines brightly and the rainbow colors paint the world so lightly. In my mind I see, a painting that might be, with water and color, my brush and my heart, stroke by stroke, my thought becomes art." As they started to paint, they were completely quiet. They knew what to do, as Donna had put the steps on the board. Many children used a circular motion to get their pumpkins round—to create the feeling of roundness. Donna talked about how to make the leaves by beginning with five-pointed star, then showed children how to create the 3-D effect by painting the curved lines on their pumpkins. (field notes)

During our interview, Donna talked about integrating the arts as more of a philosophy. Instead of presenting content straight from the book, she always asks herself how she can incorporate the arts into the presentation of the material she has to teach.

I always look at the core content, but then I dig from there what I can find that will fit.... There is always a connection. I think there are so many more avenues to take.... I think that they can then maybe paint the picture. In fact, if they're just really truly not getting the purpose of their poem, they might paint a picture and then write off of that picture. (personal interview)

Eric Jensen (2001) who has written extensively about integrating the arts into education states, "The arts enhance the process of learning. The systems they nourish, which include our integrated sensory, attentional, cognitive, emotional, and motor capacities, are, in fact, the driving forces behind all other learning" (p. 2). Besides using the visual arts to enhance their students' learning experiences, Cadre teachers, as mentioned, incorporate the fine art of storytelling.

Storytelling

Using stories to teach is an ancient tradition, and those who use storytelling in their twenty-first century classrooms insist that it is one of the finest methods to engage children's imaginations, helping them learn in a powerful way. "In storytelling, there is a coming together, a removal of boundaries, so to speak, and a total concentration and absorption of the spoken word" (Goral and Gnadinger 2006, 8). Nearly all Cadre teachers use storytelling. One referred to stories as "the drool factor." Whenever she began a story, her fourth and fifth graders' mouths hung open and they became so mesmerized they nearly drooled!

Kelly Cole said that she uses storytelling to enhance her science, math, and social studies. Although telling stories was not easy for Kelly at first, she worked on incorporating more stories into her curriculum.

> I love storytelling and I have seen what it can do, so I've been trying to use it this year. I still do not use it as much as I want to, but I've made a commitment that, starting in January, we are going to do one a week.... So I take a deep breath and say "Okay, we can do that." So one of the stories I told that I was excited about in the beginning of the year was one that I wrote about how the beeswax crayons are made.... I was very proud of myself because I was able to write a story that actually was on the first-grade level. We were learning about insects, and I was able to do a little research, and we learned all about bees. They were so excited. After the story I opened up the beeswax crayons and said "And these are the crayons." And you would have thought it was a treasure chest of gold or something; their reaction was so priceless. (personal interview)

After Kelly's success with the beeswax story, she became more confident in her ability to make and tell stories. She shared another vignette about using a book, *Bringing the Rain to Kapiti Plain* by Verna Aardema, to teach about weather. She loved the repeating lines in the book, but was worried that she could not tell the story exactly like the book, saying, "I can't tell it without the book, because I'll mess it up." So she decided to tell it herself.

> I decided to tell it my own way, without the rhyme, and it was wonderful. And we have done a guided drawing of the bees and for *Kapiti Plain*. It's amazing, the drawings they come up with. (personal interview)

Kelly said that she has to be very intentional about the way she uses Waldorf-inspired methods:

> I use the arts to make the kids take in the content more closely, personally, make more connections to the content that we have to teach.... I almost *have* to look at it that way, because I'm not really allowed to just do something for the sake of doing it. I have to have content in there somewhere. So first I know what content I have to teach, and then I think, "Okay, how can I use Waldorf to get them to get this?" (personal interview)

Donna also used storytelling extensively when teaching social studies. She discussed the power of images for the children:

> All of my fifth-grade social-studies curriculum was [taught through] storytelling. With the help of all the *History Alive* books and the *History of U.S.* books, I could read the story and sort of pick out the part I would tell them and then I would add to it.... I labored over those stories; ... the connection should be there, I mean they should feel real, like they are really in Independence Hall where [The Declaration of Independence] is being written, and the windows are closed because all of these people wanted to be a part of it. So, they are sweltering in there, because they did not want anybody to know what it was until the decisions were made. And then I go, "Wow." (personal interview)

Steiner (2000) lectured and wrote extensively about the use of storytelling as a means to connect children in a real way to the content. According to Steiner,

Educators...must make sure that the child's whole being is moved.... Try not to tell stories in a way that causes children to reflect and understand them in the head. Tell them in a way that evokes a kind of silent, thrilled awe (within limits) and in a way that evokes pleasures and sorrows that continue to echo after the child has left you, gradually to be transformed into understanding and interest. (p. 15)

The Cadre teachers could tell that storytelling went beyond delivering the content of a book or lecture. Time after time, they commented on how engaged their students were during a story.

Morning Circle

In addition to using stories to enhance learning, teachers made extensive use of the morning circle, a practice begun in schools during the 1970s in the UK (not only Waldorf schools) and imported to North America and to Waldorf schools. In the morning circle, teachers integrate songs, poetry, and movement related to the core content. Morning circle exemplifies the incorporation of Gardner's (1983) multiple intelligence theory; it uses kinesthetic intelligence, musical intelligence, linguistic intelligence, interpersonal intelligence, and intrapersonal intelligence. Some teachers even added a math circle right after lunch to help children transition from lunch and recess to classroom work. Debbie Lockyear shared this:

I started with a morning circle and then I was having some problems with math, so I started a math circle in the afternoon. It really seemed the kids really got a good foundation of things, and they enjoyed it. We would do number verses such as the "number families," and we did the clapping verse in which they do the 1 + 1 and doubles [see following pages]. (personal interview)

Donna talked about her use of the morning circle in our interview as well.

Number Family

There was a family strange indeed
Each member had a peculiar speed
They could walk for miles a day
Counting footsteps all the way
Here they come, Number 1.
[Walk and stomp on every number]
1...2...3...4...5...6...7...8...9...10...11...12
 [clap, turn around and walk and count backward]
12...11...etc.

But my two steps are not the same
For I must lean upon my cane
Although I'm tired and weak and old
I can still count with numbers bold.
 [Walk and stomp on the multiples of two]
2...4...6...8...10......24
 [clap, turn around and walk and count backward)

I'm a lad, light and free
And I'd much rather be
I can run, with my ball
And the numbers I call.
3...6...9...12...14......36
 [Clap, turn around and walk and count backward]

My step is strong
I'll not go wrong
With all my might
I'll guard what's right
I always know
Which way to go.
4...8...12...16...20.......48
 [Clap, turn around and walk and count backward]
                                    (Adaptations to verses by Mary Goral)

Since I've been through the training, I have always done circle in the morning. I have always done the movement piece...such as the number walking and poems that rhyme and poems that have rhythm. I have always done some kind of beanbag work.... We sing everyday.... It really lends itself to the multiple intelligences, which is something that we should be doing that is not only Waldorf, but it's JCPS. It's so individualizing. I never would have thought of that stuff in my first few years of teaching. Who knew? (personal interview)

Kelly Cole, too, talked about using the morning circle and how much her children loved it:

And then the other thing that I'm doing is circle. The kids love circle. If I forget about it or it doesn't happen, I hear about it. We try to go outside or to the gym to do circle, since in our classroom it's a little confined.... I usually use songs and poems that are related to the content. So then they say, "Oh, that reminds me of this," and "we made a connection." So you get to do activities where it's fun ways to get the content in. (personal interview)

Nearly all the Cadre teachers spoke of how the methods inspired by Waldorf education helped their children better understand the content. Those involved in brain research write extensively about how the brain responds to movement, music, rhythm, and rhyme. Jensen (2001) cites research indicating the value of movement in relation to learning, including the fact that more of the brain is activated during physical activity than during sedentary activity.

Understanding Concepts

According to the information from Jensen, when students are taught in ways that help them understand and remember concepts, teachers realize the significance of this and try to incorporate these methods into as many of their daily activities as possible. The more they use, the easier it gets for them. Furthermore, teachers find that the children who often fail to grasp certain ideas and concepts understand

DOUBLES VERSE
by Jenny Heath

One and one is two
Just like me and you.
Two and two are four
I can still do more.
Three and three make six
Throw that in the mix.
Four and four are eight
I think that is great.
Five and five are ten
Let's continue then.

them better when they are brought to them through these methods. Kelly shared the following:

It's not just because it's fun, exciting, and all of that. It's also that there are probably a couple of kids who are not going to get it unless I go that way. So I guess, besides the fact that I'm excited about being a good teacher when I do that, there are kids that may not be—it might not be simple for them until that happens. (personal interview)

During a conversation about Waldorf main-lesson books, Jan spoke about understanding concepts, in particular, depth of understanding:

It was not so much the pictures in the main-lesson books that were so beautiful, but that they had so much depth, so much comprehension, and so much width of understanding. It seemed like there was so much more in the work itself than what you normally see kind of fluffed out by children. And there was thoughtfulness; there was inspiration; there was just a sense of the child having been touched and inspired. (personal interview)

Given the depth of understanding and inspiration she witnessed, Jan has tried to include a significant amount of Waldorf-inspired teaching in her art room.

> If I am teaching something, I want them to comprehend; usually they will do some kind of movement and song or rhythm, or there will be a story.... Every once in a while, we will have a child sort of opt out. I can almost guarantee you...that child will be the one who cannot do the drawing that we have done in terms of bodily movement. They literally cannot. It has gotten to the point of explaining, "If you do not do it with your big muscles, it is much harder to bring it into your small ones."... It seems like there has been this little light that goes on. (personal interview)

Jan talked about how she has grown in her ability to integrate rhythm and movement to help teach difficult concepts to her students, as well as how her students have helped in writing songs and poems to enrich a concept:

> Previously, I would have to write it down—you know, different steps, different words to mention at each step. And now it's as if it is embedded within me. I know I am going to pick up on those important steps, but the children are going to bring in even more, enrich that even more.... The second verse of the rainbow song came from a child...I could not think for the life of me how to rhyme the secondary colors...and a little girl came up with the secondary scheme— orange, purple, secondary scheme, regular blue, primary hue—and so we do this little song and dance thing to that. And it was just so much easier. They just so get it. (personal interview)

Shawna Stenton, who also teaches at Jeffersontown Elementary, spoke of how her integration of Waldorf-inspired methods helps her students understand certain science concepts:

We incorporate art because it engages the students. For example, watercolors come at the end of the year, and we do that with our weather unit, because you can make the paintings with the sun and the moon...that's something they understand.... Also, when they blend the two colors, I have them do sunrises and sunsets so they can see the weather around them in that. When I introduce [the sun and moon] to them in watercolors, I tell them a story, but it will be more about the colors and how they play together. And then at the end they say, "Oh, I made a moon, I made a sun." That's making that connection. (personal interview)

Cadre teachers have been able to integrate many aspects of Waldorf education, from storytelling to morning circle, to the arts. From my observations and interviews, it is clear that the more they tried Waldorf-inspired pedagogy, the more comfortable they felt and the more engaged their students became. Not only were their students more engaged in the teaching and learning process, but student understanding also increased. By continually delving more deeply into Waldorf-inspired teaching, Cadre members go beyond "best practices." They do what Steven Wolk (2007) so passionately calls for: "We must rethink our classrooms as vibrant spaces that awaken consciousness to the world, open minds to the problems of our human condition, inspire wonder, and help people to lead personally fulfilling lives" (p. 658).

LOVING SCHOOL

As part of Steiner's first lecture from *Practical Advice to Teachers* (2000), he says, "Our task is to find teaching methods that continually engage the whole human being" (p. 5). Steiner elaborates that teachers must infuse their teaching with heart and soul and must not "offer children understanding merely for their ears, but...communicate from soul to soul. If you remember this, you will make progress" (p. 16). Working closely with Cadre teachers over the years, I have witnessed the depth of the relationships they have developed with their students and the way students react to these teachers. I have heard numerous stories of how grateful parents are to Cadre teachers for their dedication and commitment. Teachers have also shared with me the challenges they've faced in attempting to infuse Waldorf-inspired methods into their public-school classrooms. Despite these challenges, they continue to inspire and engage their students.

Student Engagement

Rachel Kessler (2000) writes that, when we bring heart and soul into our teaching, we have to redefine participation and emphasize "engagement and attentiveness rather than talking and doing" (p. 52). Given comments from conversations with Cadre members, I found this to be true. Many teachers discussed their students' engagement in terms of the "looks on their faces," or how still they were, or how they never complained. Few, if any, discussed, as Kessler says, "talking and doing." Debbie Lockyear shared her experiences with storytelling and her students' responses:

> With the storytelling, it amazes me because there are only one or two children maybe who are not sitting there wide-eyed and watching with anticipation and excitement.... It always is interesting that they are so engaged.... It's different to have those Waldorf activities because the children do get engaged and they are really loving it. (personal interview)

Kelly Cole also related how her little first graders responded to storytelling:

> They change when I'm telling a story without a book. And every time I do it, I cannot get enough of it.... For instance, I have some students who are always well-behaved; they always sit on their bottoms; they never talk; they always listen to what they are told; they do everything right; but they have not had this [storytelling]. And when I tell them these stories, I watch their faces...their eyes light up, they're smiling. These are kids who are maybe not smiling very often. They are excited.... And the

ones who kind of goof off a little, they get excited probably more than they are supposed to. I have to say "No." I have to calm them down. But they're excited about what I'm teaching. They're not goofing off.... I also told a story for math time the other day. It was about a lion that throws a spear. They have a contest about throwing the spear, and I could not find the book in the library, so it forced me to tell it.... I wrote it down for myself. I walked around the room and told the story to them, and...the looks on their faces, they got excited. (personal interview)

These comments from Kelly contain an interesting twist. Most teachers speak of how storytelling engages their children, especially those who are normally wiggly and distracted. But rarely do they talk about how Waldorf methods affect children who are always good, who are always on task. This type of engagement derived from Waldorf-inspired teaching touches children in a way that traditional teaching does not. The look of awe and wonder on children's faces, the smiles and the excitement, this is teaching that goes beyond so-called best practices and truly educates the whole child.

Donna talked about her first experience of using Waldorf-inspired teaching in her classroom and her students' reactions to storytelling. When she was teaching third grade at Greenwood Elementary, she remembers singing "The Dandelion Song" (see next page) and telling a story about the number four. She then used images from the number four to teach the fours multiplication table. According to Donna,

The kids were so totally with it. And that storytelling thing—when they get into that "coma," they are with you. So that was it. I just started incorporating more and more of the methods. (personal interview)

Mona Jones shared a story about her experience with her students at the end of the last school year. They were reviewing the year together, and Mona asked them to relate the most meaningful thing they had learned during the year. She said that many of her students shared how much they loved painting and drawing. However, one of her students

was especially touched by the stories she told: "One of my smartest little boys—his mother had died…he's real little and still talks with a lisp—he said 'I loved your storytelling'" (personal interview).

Storytelling has a soul quality that reading from a book or lecturing does not capture. It is pure connection, one person to another, with nothing in between. Jan spoke about this inherent quality in Waldorf-inspired teaching:

I used to attempt to bring in those words, those terms [artistic elements], but it is almost like dry toast versus toast with jelly and whipped cream.... It is a whole different thing. Even though I would attempt to be very enthusiastic—to teach in a rote way, that's all you have. If you get them up and moving and dancing and singing, they get it, number one, immediately. And number two; they enjoy being able to move. (personal interview)

The principals that I interviewed had a different view on student engagement. Kris Raitzer noticed that students talked about this outside of class:

The kids would say, "Oh, we get to do fun things that the other kids don't get to do." And the kids talked about those different kinds of activities that they had never gotten to do before. (personal interview)

Not only were kids more engaged and excited about school, Cadre members noted that the quality of students' work also increased.

Quality of Work

When I taught in the public schools, I used to do a lot of creative activities with my students. They wrote plays, made tiny villages when studying Native American tribes, wrote and performed songs, read novels about the era of history we were studying, and participated in math and science projects. However, there was always something missing. At the time, I did not know what it was. When I discovered Waldorf education, I knew that the missing piece was a more reverent approach to the earth and to everything they did, including the quality of their work. Students often rushed through assignments and handed in poorly done work that was messy and incorrect. Sometimes I was so relieved to get any work from them that I accepted it. Other times I knew it was not their best work, but I didn't know how to evoke this kind of work from them. Attention to aesthetics, to the beauty and wonder of life, must surround children on a daily and moment-to-moment basis. When children are in an environment such as this, the quality of their work begins to reflect it. As teachers, we begin to expect and even demand it.

Patty Gilderbloom discussed this in relation to the children in her classroom who had an IEP (Individualized Educational Program):

> In particular, I saw profound changes, even in the kids who perhaps were labeled as the slower learners in the class. Some of those children had the most beautiful artwork in the whole class. (personal interview)

Debbie Lockyear saw a tremendous improvement in the quality of her students' work, particularly in their handwriting and in their ability to add detail to their writing:

> The storytelling, I found that with practice. I would tell the story, and then I would let the kids practice retelling parts to me. During our writing time, when I looked at other classes and their writing, I found that a lot of my kids were adding so much more detail, being able to use language [from the stories].... Actually, we would hang up some of their writing in the hall, and people were always so impressed with how they were writing. I think it [storytelling] gave them a better sense of written language because they understood how to formulate descriptive language in their heads and talk about it. (personal interview)

The rich language used in storytelling appeals to students in a way that language "at their level" does not. Although most kindergarten and first-grade students cannot read the more difficult, descriptive vocabulary used in a beautiful fairy tale, they can certainly understand it, many times extracting the meaning from the context.

Debbie shared how she worked with her students on handwriting skills. As in many private Waldorf-schools, Cadre members working with children in the primary grades implemented the "earth, grass, and sky" technique, using brown, green, and blue block crayons to set up their paper to guide their writing.

Earth, grass, and sky technique

When we practiced writing our letters, we did the earth, grass, and sky. At first, my aide did not know what I was doing. She finally told me that this was the class that had the best writing skills. Their development was incredible. (personal interview)

During a visit to Donna Stottman's classroom, I noticed all of the beautiful aesthetic touches she had added to her space, including a lovely chalk drawing on the board and a poem:

APPLE SECRETS

Who would think an apple
Red, gold, or green
And round
Would have a secret
Deep inside
That when cut
It can be found.

Donna commented on the effects she thought Waldorf-inspired teaching had on her students:

They have become more observant. I don't know if that is just because of Waldorf methods, but there's so much nature....

I try to add a little something to the nature table or change something to the chalk drawing or move something around, and so I always start my year with that.... Then Tyler said this year, "You love nature. You always have cool nature stuff, like the window with whatever is there—the flowers or the picture." The setting [in my room] is usually beautiful, so I think it's cool when they notice. (personal interview)

Donna noted a connection with this attention to detail in the classroom and her students' writing. She wasn't certain, but believed there is a definite link between her students' increased powers of observation and attention to detail in the classroom and their generous use of detail in their writing. Not only have teachers noticed a difference in their students' work and engagement, but parents, too, have noticed changes in their children.

Parental Reactions

According to Zemelman, Daniels, and Hyde (1998), most parents across the country passively accept today's skill-based approach to learning, which resembles the education that they received:

It seems that the only approaches to schooling that American parents ever advocate for passionately are those that take meaning out of the center of the curriculum; and the only kinds of schooling they oppose, in any organized fashion, are those that allow kids to hear, discuss, and grapple with major ideas and values of our culture. (pp. 194–195)

Zemelman et al. further explain that, in order to help parents accept this different, deeper understanding of exploring content, they began to offer workshops for parents, which they found to be very successful.

Most assuredly, we often hear from parents when their children are struggling or when they disagree with a teacher's innovative pedagogy. Yet I disagree that this is the only time parents voice their opinions. In my experience while working with the Cadre, parents of their students have stepped forward on a number of occasions to let Cadre teachers know how much they appreciate what these teachers are bringing to their children.

Donna and Tina shared parents' poignant stories about changes they noticed in their children. The parent of a young boy in their class had been extremely worried about the fact that her son was not athletic. However, she began to notice that her son was happier than he had ever been, and attributed it to the fact that Donna and Tina integrated music and art into their classrooms on a daily basis. According to Donna, this child "is loving life." She is happy that he has it as an outlet (personal interview).

Another story from Donna involves an end-of-the-year project that her students put together and the parents' reactions to the project:

> Every child at the end of the fourth grade had a painting, a handwork piece, a verse, and a written piece.... I got four bulletin boards, so it was just a hallway of black background and all of that color. And I had a whole bunch of people ask me about it.... I had a parent say (he got teary), "I don't know what you do in your classroom, but you have touched my son." And he started crying, and his wife started crying. So it's really powerful. They see that it's different. (personal interview)

This difference parents sense often translates into teacher requests. Most Cadre teachers have more parent requests than they can handle. Mona said, "I had a lot of requests this year...because of the artistic work I bring to the kids" (personal interview). Not only do parents request Cadre teachers, they also communicate with the teachers and let them know how much their students love school.

Tina related a story about the number of transfers from other schools and how parents responded:

> Most of it has been positive. And most of them [parents] have come up and said, or written us a note that says, "My child loves school this year. This is the first time." (personal interview)

Cadre teachers also notice the difference. A number of Mona's students go home and tell their parents what they are learning in school.

All the parents tell me that they [the children] come home from school and talk about school, and they play school all weekend. Well, how many children go home and talk about school? (personal interview)

CONCLUSION

Although Cadre teachers are highly enthusiastic about the Waldorf-inspired methods that they are able to include in their classrooms, as well as the increased engagement and quality of work witnessed in their students, many also spoke of the challenges involved in taking up this form of teaching. Teachers say that it is hard, certainly more work than handing out worksheets. Often, the demands from the district are such that it is just too much to do it all.

Over the five years since I took over the Cadre project, a number of teachers have dropped out. They assured me that it is not my leadership style, but that, because of the increased demands of NCLB and the extreme translation of that law by JCPS, there is no time to do anything "extra."

Yet, the teachers who remained in the Cadre have continued to find ways to integrate Waldorf-inspired teaching into their classrooms. By going beyond best practices through a deep integration of the arts, student engagement and love of learning have increased. As a result, teachers know that this type of education is not only meaningful for their students, but also necessary for their own growth as educators. Many talk about how this way of teaching has changed their lives and kept them in the teaching profession.

5

THE INNER LIFE OF THE TEACHER

*"We all know that what will transform education is not another theory, another book, or another formula but educators who are willing to seek a transformed way of being in the world."
(Parker Palmer 1999, 14)*

MOST INDIVIDUALS GO INTO TEACHING for reasons of the heart and, in a purely metaphysical way, are "called" to teach. They have an inner desire to change the world. They love children, love the way they feel when they are with children, or as Bill Ayers (1993) puts it, "They become teachers because they love the world enough that they want to show that love to others.... I teach in the hope of making the world a better place" (p. 8). However, something happens along the way that drains well-meaning teachers of that initial passion for teaching and learning. Matthew Fox (2006) believes our educational system is stuck in the modern tradition of seeking knowledge, rather than seeking meaning. Because we live in a postmodern world, it is crucial that we extract ourselves from "miseducation to mindful education" (Fox 2006, 27). Those who write about the infusion of spirituality into education call for an opening of the heart, so that we may once again instill meaning, wonder, and awe into the education of our children. Before education can truly change, however, educators must change the way they live, move, and have their being in and out of the classroom. "What we seek is a way of working illumined by spirit and infused with soul," says Parker Palmer (1999, 15).

"How can educational institutions sustain and deepen the selfhood from which good teaching comes?" asks Samuel Intrator (2002, 155). Through Intrator's work with Parker Palmer's Courage to Teach program, he has found that attention to the inner life can make the difference between teachers dropping out and teachers becoming revitalized in their work and rededicated to the profession. Similar in intent to Palmer's Courage to Teach, the teachers involved in the Waldorf-inspired Cadre have found renewed meaning in their work. Cadre teachers related that their work with Waldorf-inspired pedagogy and methods has not only kept them in teaching, but has also changed and deepened their teaching. Furthermore, Cadre teachers continually seek to learn more and expand their understanding of teaching. This chapter focuses on the inner lives of the Cadre teachers and tells stories of the way Waldorf education renewed their passion for teaching and deepened their commitment to the profession.

LIFELONG LEARNING

What is it that makes some educators seek new ways of reaching their students, while others are content with the status quo and merely doing what they can with the limited resources at hand? I am continually impressed by teachers who self-select to learn more, who seek new ways of relating to their students to deepen their understanding of teaching. Teachers in the Waldorf-inspired Cadre were not forced or recruited to bring this type of pedagogy to their students. Most found out about the Cadre by asking questions, and most asked questions because they were not satisfied with their current situation. Similar to my earlier research conducted with private Waldorf-school teachers, I found that the teachers in the study "felt there was something missing" either in their early education or in the work they were doing prior to teaching in a Waldorf school. This "something missing" refers to the lack of attention given to the wholeness of the human being" (Sturbaum 1997,

56). By self-selecting, teachers clearly wanted more for their students as well as for themselves.

Self Selection

As noted, most people go into teaching because they want to make a difference in the world. The profession is self-selecting by nature. However, those interested in Waldorf education seem to be drawn to it in an exceptionally powerful way. Many say that they finally found what they had been searching for, and some teachers even admit to the feeling of "coming home." Patty Gilderbloom, a former teacher at Byck Elementary, stated that she finally found a name to put with what she believed to be the best kind of teaching:

> It's been quite a journey.... I have been grasping at straws ever since I began teaching in 1985; because even when I was teaching back then, I was doing so much of what Waldorf methodology is, but not really knowing what I was doing or that it even had a name. I think it is a natural process. I don't think everyone can be or wants to be a Waldorf teacher.... When I first found the methods...and saw other people doing the things that I had been doing, but not knowing that I was doing Waldorf, it was such a revelation. (personal interview)

Shannon Conlon, a former principal at Byck Elementary, spoke about this process of self-selection and pointed out the importance of letting teachers come to Waldorf rather than pushing them into it:

> When I think of Waldorf, I do not feel that there is anybody out there selling it or recruiting; it's that you don't come to them—they come to you.... I found that I have pushed it at times, recruited it at times.... And when you recruit it takes something out of it [Waldorf-inspired teaching]. You cannot make people something they are not. And so, I am understanding. I would say that something I did learn is not to recruit. And I guess maybe [I learned about] my impatience. That it takes a long time for somebody to come to you. (personal interview)

Shannon found out through trial and error that not everyone was meant to be, or wanted to be, part of the Cadre. She also realized that, for some teachers, it was a natural fit and that Waldorf-inspired pedagogy actually became a part of who they were.

> You can tell the ones that really have it. I mean, it seems natural. They are really one with their kids. And it extends into the community. It's not a job from 9:05 to 3:45. It's all a part of them. If it doesn't flow or feel a part of them, it feels artificial. And then I think the lifestyle extends beyond the classroom.... You just cannot [say] "Okay, I am at work today, so I am going to do that and then I am going to go back to the other ways." It bleeds into your whole life. I don't think people really see that. (personal interview)

Research on school reform has shown that teachers involved in a particular school movement or philosophy have a level of commitment not always found in traditional settings (Wood 1993). Jan Kovac, teacher at Jeffersontown Elementary, shared the following:

> Waldorf has become a part of my life. So I think about that a lot. If I have a problem, I go back to some of the knowledge that I've received through Waldorf. And my application [of the pedagogy] has been building layer-by-layer. I have noticed I am just getting better and better and pulling more and more into my teaching. (personal interview)

Thirsty for Knowledge

Some teachers will pull out the same lesson plans year after year and seem perfectly satisfied with that way of teaching. Members of the Cadre, however, would never fall into that category. These men and women continuously seek new ways of presenting information to their children; they love learning for its own sake and see gathering new skills and ideas as something that feeds their souls, helping to recharge them for their day-to-day work. In Steiner's final lecture to the teachers in the first Waldorf school, he made these concluding remarks:

I would like for you to stick firmly to the following four principles.... The teacher must be a person of initiative in everything done, great and small.... The teacher should be one who is interested in the being of the whole world and of humanity.... The teacher must be one who never compromises in the heart and mind with what is untrue.... The teacher must never get stale or grow sour. (2000, 187–188)

Although principal Kris Raitzer did not use Steiner's words to describe her Waldorf-inspired team, her sentiments regarding these teachers could definitely be compared to the principles Steiner upheld for his original teachers.

Because they are Waldorf-inspired or trained teachers in the public schools, they need to be true learners themselves. They are... intellectually intrigued by the process of learning and how to make learning better, how to make kids more academically successful. And they are just so much fun to talk to, because they ask good questions. And they ponder things. They will be my teachers who will challenge what we do. (personal interview)

Teachers shared stories about finding poetry, music, and stories to use with their students and how they practiced and worked to make sure that they were bringing materials that were developmentally appropriate, as well as meaningful.

When I was first starting to paint, I painted every week myself, trying to figure out what it was going to be like. I'd find a picture in a book and think, "Okay, how do I make this real for kids?" Or when we did "The Midnight Ride of Paul Revere," I thought, "Now, what is the image we are going to be able to paint?... There is a lot of detail in that story." I find myself trying things and smushing my brush around and thinking, "How am I going to explain this to kids?" (personal interview)

Cadre teachers seek to make their students more successful academically, and they seek to make their own lives more fulfilling, as well.

Self-nurturing through Learning

According to Sam Intrator (2002), teaching is a calling that requires constant renewal of the spirit, heart, and mind. In The Courage to Teach program, Intrator works with K–12 educators. In the program, teachers meet seasonally at three-day retreats, where they focus not on school reform or technique, but on their inner lives. In large or small group settings, the inner life of the teacher is explored through personal stories and reflections, as well as through poetry, music, and storytelling (Intrator 2002). The workshops and classes with the Waldorf-inspired Cadre involve this type of inner work. Professional development focuses on the arts as a means to nurture teachers' spirits. According to Conte (2001), "I am awed by the power of the arts to nurture human beings and provide transformational, community-enhancing experiences" (p. 78). Teachers spoke openly of their appreciation for this work. Donna commented:

> I think my professional development had always been "you read about it"; but with our Cadre, we got to *do* it, and that is what I love. If I can see it, I can make it my own, generally. And who doesn't want to cross-stitch and say "I made this for you." (personal interview)

Teachers appreciate the nature of the workshops and actually crave the work when they have been away from it. Debbie Lockyear said that she had to miss our two-week institute one year because of her graduate work.

> Because I was missing out on the Waldorf Institute, I focused my graduate project on Waldorf storytelling so I could learn more about the storytelling and how that helps kids with their oral language. (personal interview)

Before the two-week summer institute in Louisville (mentioned in chapter 2), teachers traveled to Rudolf Steiner College near Sacramento for their institute on Waldorf methods applied in the public-school setting. Mona Jones spoke about her experience in California and how our institute filled that need for her.

> After the two years that I went [to Rudolf Steiner College], I just craved the institute. And it lasted for only two years! So, fortunately we had the Cadre, and we got to go and share some things.... Sometimes we would have painting lessons with Janey, but I was missing the institute so badly. And when it started here at Bellarmine, I took the art part, and it blew me away. I was so happy that we had this same kind of thing going on right here. (personal interview)

Principal Shannon Conlon talked about the importance of our workshops and classes in helping to energize her teachers:

> They get their energy and motivation and new ideas [from the workshops]. I think that people see the benefit and want more.... I see the teachers who really buy into this whole thing. They are the ones who give me information, "Here is an article, here is this to share." (personal interview)

Often, when teachers were working on new material for their children, they found that this digging for information ultimately led to a revitalization in their own interests. Tina said that she had found a poetry book in the Chicago airport for her children and that this began to enhance her own interest in poetry: "I bought it for them; I read it for the kids, but I like it, too. So maybe I am reading it for myself" (personal interview).

Brenda talked about how writing for herself, which she did at Rudolf Steiner College, was so powerful.

> Connecting to writing really has been huge for me, that connection between writing and what I learned in California was powerful. It really helped me, because I want to grow in my own writing. (personal interview)

Many of the teachers spoke of how they would like to do more artistic work for themselves, but often they lack the time. Donna noted:

I would like to learn drumming. I would like to learn recorder.
I did the veil painting with Janey. [Even] she said "I just do not
paint by myself. I have to make myself do it." It's just one more
thing. (personal interview)

Finally, a number of teachers have deepened their inner lives
through the study of Anthroposophy, Rudolf Steiner's path to personal development. In our program, we offer elective-study courses in
Anthroposophy, and the teachers who opt to investigate this spiritual
science, which in reality undergirds all of Steiner's work, have found it
to be quite powerful. Patty Gilderbloom shared:

I think it is possibly through the Anthroposophy courses that
I feel I am doing more inward teaching and, in a sense, looking
at the children quite differently from the other years. (personal
interview)

Through a variety of experiences, Cadre teachers have developed and
deepened their inner lives. Individuals already on the path of personal
development are drawn to Waldorf education. It is more than merely
teaching to the intellect. It is more than delivering content to students.
Waldorf education requires teachers to look inward and to continue
their own learning. Cadre teachers are seekers. Angeles Arrien (2002)
contends, "As we move into the twenty-first century, it is the work of
all human beings to attend to the health of both our 'inner' and 'outer'
houses: the inner house of ourselves, the limitless world within, and
the outer house of the world in which we live our daily lives" (p. 148).
Such attention to their inner "houses" has helped teachers develop the
"outer" world of their teaching.

Deepened Pedagogy

"We are in search of a pedagogy of experience and participation, a
pedagogy both situated in and stretching beyond itself, a critical pedagogy capable of questioning, rethinking, reimagining" (Ayers 2004,
84). Bill Ayres captures the essence of Cadre teachers' search for a more
engaging style of teaching. Some teachers attribute their growth to a

more spiritual approach to teaching, whereas others credit their change to a stronger understanding of the development of the child. Through this growth in their teaching, they have found the courage to remain in the classroom. Ayres (2004), again encourages us through his heart-felt prose: "We can look inside our selves, summon strength we never knew we had, connect up with other teachers and parents and kids to create the schools and classrooms we deserve" (p. 143). Through their study of Anthroposophy, child development, and a methodology that meets the needs of their students, Cadre members continue to deepen their teaching and enliven their classrooms.

Growth through Anthroposophy

Steiner frequently emphasized that the Waldorf approach is more than the application of a certain teaching method. "This new art of education was born out of a solid anthroposophic foundation, out of the knowledge of the growing child as body, soul, and spirit" (Steiner 1983, viii). Whether one must be an anthroposophist to be a Waldorf teacher remains an unresolved question, even in the private Waldorf-school settings. However, it certainly enhances the probability that teachers will meditate and reflect on issues of spiritual growth. I have found that teachers who undertake the study of Anthroposophy believe their understanding of the child has deepened. According to Patty Gilderbloom,

> Last year, when I started reading Anthroposophy and ways of looking at the child and ways of looking at child development, and really understanding the essence of the child and how they learn and how they grow, and stages of child development according to Rudolf Steiner, then that made me become more of an aware teacher. I believe that makes my teaching stronger. But it is just a process of growth. And every year and every class and every time I read more Steiner, it just accentuates my teaching and deepens my understanding of the human being, and how important it is not only to look at the mind, but to look at the heart and the soul of every child as well. (personal interview)

Not all Cadre teachers have taken up the study of Anthroposophy, but many recognized the benefits of a spiritual approach to teaching. There is definitely a deep satisfaction that comes in knowing you are working from a soul place with your students. Debbie Lockyear spoke about how using Waldorf-inspired pedagogy grounded her and calmed her in times of stress:

> Waldorf helps the teachers as much as it helps the students. It helps us stay grounded; it gives us some peace. Sometimes, when I was at the end of my patience level, just singing a transition song—even if the kids were ignoring me and they were too rowdy to sing along—gave me that ability to get a little calmer and more peaceful. Eventually they would come along and start doing it. But I think it gave me a lot of peace and helpfulness during the situation.... It gives me a lot more peace and energy at the end of the day, too.... I think that is one of the very large parts of my growth. (personal interview)

Other teachers spoke of their work with Waldorf education and how it has led them to a deeper, more thorough knowledge of child development. Unfortunately, in traditional schools of education, the study of child development is isolated from curriculum and pedagogy. Teachers are not equipped to understand why students do certain things at certain times, and they can become frustrated when their kids are unable to learn. When teachers are given an opportunity to delve more deeply into child development, in particularly Steiner's theory of child development, they begin to understand how to bring content to children in ways that they can relate to, understand, and sustain.

Understanding Child Development

According to Steiner (2000), "To find the right curriculum for children ages seven to fourteen or fifteen is bound up in general with a true knowledge of child development over this period of time" (p. 106). One of the biggest dilemmas facing teachers today is the increased governmental expectations for children ages seven to fourteen. Owing to the erroneous and ill-conceived NCLB law, students are no longer given the luxury of learning concepts when they are developmentally ready for them. Instead, they are *all* expected to reach "proficiency" in their academic subjects by particular, arbitrary grade levels. This ridiculous mandate has teachers tearing their hair out, because all of the children cannot possibly learn and master, for example, algebraic thinking in kindergarten. Although Cadre teachers must, by law, teach the core content to their students, they have the advantage of a more thorough understanding of child development and are at least able to bring inappropriate subject matter to their students in more developmentally appropriate ways. The following story illustrates this.

A first-grade teacher at Byck Elementary was struggling with the fact that she had to teach fractions to her young students. According to Steiner's educational principles, the appropriate time to teach fractions is only after children have gone through the nine-year change, as this is the time when a child's self, or "I"-consciousness, is strengthened and consolidated (Steiner 2000, 106). In other words, before the age of nine, children are not really separate from the world; it is all one big unity. After the age of nine, however, they begin to distinguish themselves more from their surroundings (Steiner 2000). This being said, how can children separate a number into parts if they cannot separate their own individuality from the world around them?

Because children in first grade are in the developmental phase of imagination, the teacher might teach fractions through a fairy tale. Together we worked on creating a story that took the archetypal characters from a traditional fairy tale, and wove in some basic concepts of fractions (see appendix, "The Fraction Story"). I modeled the telling of the story to her children. They sat in rapt attention, eyes big as saucers, mouths agape. Later, after we had let the story rest, we drew a picture together that illustrated the concept the teacher needed to convey. Because the fact that the children were able to form mental pictures from the feeling realm rather than from their intellect, they were able to better grasp the concept and retain it.

Donna spoke in detail about her first experience of Steiner's approach to child development, which happened at the first Waldorf-inspired workshop she attended. Fortunately for her, the speaker was

Betty Staley, a Waldorf educator and author from Rudolf Steiner College. Donna spoke of her introduction to Steiner's theory of child development:

> With her [Betty's] knowledge of child development and all of the seven-year cycles, all of that was just really glow in the dark to me. I thought—finally—somebody who can tell me why this kid does this. And so from there I just came to whatever [workshop] I could find. (personal interview)

Brenda was teaching in the same school as Donna, across the hall in fact. She was struggling with her students in her special-education class.

> I always felt so responsible when my students didn't get it. I never felt like, "Well it's his fault; if he would just..." It was always like, "What am I doing wrong? What do I need to do?" What we had wasn't working.... I saw that she [Donna] was meeting kids' needs, and I wasn't.... I saw her and how they were responding to her, and I couldn't even hear her. I think demeanor, too. You become a little different in yourself. I think all these questions go together because you become different yourself. I mean just the way you talk to kids and the way you see them differently. I thought, I have to do that, especially I want to reach the hard ones. The ones that couldn't, aren't making it. (personal interview)

James Comer (1998) believes that despite the massive changes in our society, the needs of children have remained basically the same. Comer (1998) contends that children perhaps need an even higher level of development than in the past:

> Too many children are not receiving the kind of development they need to go to school, and too many go to school underdeveloped, alienated, and psychologically hurt. On the other side, too many schools are unprepared to support the development of these children or to bring them to a level of necessary development. (p. 8)

Comer challenges schools of education to look more deeply into issues of child development and to move away from theoretical, abstract courses disconnected from the real world. Steiner's thorough approach to teaching through a developmentally appropriate curriculum has helped a number of Cadre teachers reach children they had previously been unable to reach. Jan Kovac describes how she's changed her teaching and made it more accessible to her students. Not only does she use developmentally appropriate strategies, she also makes sure to bring the material to children in a variety of different modalities:

> Previously, when I taught I would find a project, and I would present each step to the children, and it would drive me crazy that a lot of them didn't get the steps, even though they were broken down.... But it wasn't brought in to the different modalities of learning. I didn't understand why they weren't getting it, because I thought, "What else am I supposed to do here? I've done everything visually that I possibly can do." But Waldorf, of course, preceded Gardner's multiple intelligences and the different ways of learning by years. So, literally, I'm taking their refined approach; I've been able to do that and just bring in all of that richness.... Before, I was very limited in my scope of abilities, and my creativity as well. It gave me a whole box of watercolors. It took me into so many different modes of learning as well as teaching. (personal interview)

Kelly Cole, too, spoke of how her work with Waldorf education has helped her differentiate the curriculum for her students.

> It's making me think more deeply about how I am going to get the information across to them, the whole differentiation [process]; they all learn differently. I think it's almost my responsibility to make sure that I am going at the same content in different ways. And so Waldorf has helped me have one more way to reach kids who need that way. (personal interview)

Although child development, the theory of multiple intelligences, and differentiating the curriculum are actually three separate concepts in the field of education, having a strong grasp of each obviously helps teachers reach their children in ways that traditional approaches to teaching do not. As Kelly stated, implementing a Waldorf-inspired approach to teaching is one more way to help her get through to those children who may be more difficult to reach. Furthermore, all three methods of teaching ultimately enhance teachers' creativity.

Jan, an artist and a creative person to begin with, noted that Waldorf education has helped her develop an "enormous creative flow":

> I look at the creative flow. I see that source of energy as being behind these windows. And if you can crack the window a little bit, that flow will start to come, and it will start to push the window open more and more and more. Pretty soon, the window is always open, and you are just drawing on that. A lot of times, I'll be teaching something and all of a sudden, out of the blue, I will have this poem come out of my mouth that catches the concept. I'm trying to convey a little ditty that just kind of hits me.... It comes very naturally now. It really flows through me.... Teaching has become a great joy, whereas before it was more tedious. (personal interview)

Jan concluded our interview by expounding more on her appreciation for the Waldorf-inspired work in which she feels so fortunate to have been involved:

> It just gets better and better and better all of the time. This has been such a gift. I wish classroom teachers could understand how much more enriching and fulfilling, inspiring and exciting it is to work within this technique. Even though it might be more difficult work in terms of creating your curriculum, my gosh—it's just night and day when it comes to working out of a textbook versus working out of your creative source.... It's made a huge difference for me. (personal interview)

Jan's sentiments regarding how her teaching has changed and how in fact it has become more joyous was echoed by a number of Cadre members. In fact, many Cadre teachers admitted that their Waldorf-inspired work has kept them in the profession.

Renewed Joy

As we move further into the reality of education in the twenty-first century, many teachers face a teaching career devoid of meaning. As mentioned, most teachers go into the profession for reasons of the heart and a strong desire to serve society and help children. However, according to Intrator (2002), "Reality is often the opposite.... We become bitter and disillusioned and feel victimized by the system" (p.18). The politics of teaching, coupled with increased expectations from society, have caused many teachers to lose heart and leave the profession for more lucrative and less "frustrating" work. For others, teaching becomes just a job—something to do from nine to three, "a strict exchange of time for money" (Rockne in Intrator 2002, 20). It is hard to say which is worse—great teachers who leave the profession, or great teachers who stay and are no longer engaged or engaging.

Nonetheless, some educators, through their own efforts or through pure happenstance, find a way to renew their joy and to reconnect with their original passion with increased wisdom, wonder, and a softened heart. Programs on a national scale, such as Parker Palmer's Courage to Teach, and others on a much smaller level, such as our Waldorf-inspired Cadre, have enabled teachers to find the strength to continue teaching. By focusing on the teachers themselves, both programs have helped teachers reconnect to the heart and soul of teaching through a renewed sense of community. According to Palmer (2002), "Through community, teachers can become more engaged in the processes that shape education, can become leaders in helping transform the settings of our professional and political lives" (p. 315).

Nearly all of the teachers interviewed spoke about the importance the Cadre community played in keeping them in teaching. Tina Marsteller had been a member of a Waldorf-inspired team at Dixie Elementary with Patty Rundell, Barbara Doyle, and Jennifer Geroski. When the principal at Dixie left for another position, the team wanted to leave with her. But because of the transfer rules in JCPS, this did not happen.

Tina was left on her own for a year or two before she transferred to Blue Lick Elementary, where Donna Stottman and Brenda Chelliah were teaching.

> It is really different when you're on your own. And I've been in transition. I don't know how long the transition is going to last, but I'm in a good transition. So I feel I am sort of waking up again. (personal interview)

Tina's reawakening had to do with the fact that she was once again with other Cadre members. When Donna first transferred to Blue Lick, she was also on her own. She felt frustrated by this experience as well.

> When I was the only person that first year at Blue Lick, which would have been four years ago, a primary teacher came to me and said, "Waldorf—I heard they say prayers to the sun; that's against my religion." And so I debunked the myth. But, how do you explain it [Waldorf] to somebody who has already decided it is not for her? (personal interview)

Debbie Lockyear had a similar experience when she transferred from Byck to Hartstern Elementary:

> Then I ventured out to Hartstern, where Kelly Cole forged a little bit of an effort the year before. And she went in delicately. And she said that I let my Waldorf freak flag fly. She said "If you wouldn't let that freak flag fly so high, people wouldn't give you such a hard time here." But to me, it has to fly because it's got to be a part of the classroom. I went in with a bang, but it met the needs of my kids. (personal interview)

Strength definitely comes in numbers. Having Debbie at Hartstern actually gave Kelly courage to implement more Waldorf-inspired pedagogy in her classroom. Donna also talked about how difficult it is to be the only person using a Waldorf-inspired pedagogy, and how wonderful it was when Brenda and Tina came to Blue Lick. Brenda believed that her coming to Blue Lick was meant to be:

We were meant to be together. We were meant to be in the same building. We were meant to find each other.... I did not want to be at Blue Lick, but here I am. (personal interview)

As of 2009, Cadre teachers had found principals at several schools who welcome the Waldorf-inspired approach to teaching: Lowe Elementary had three Cadre members; Byck had a Waldorf-inspired team with a Cadre teacher at each grade level; Hartstern had two Cadre teachers; Chenoweth, two; Jeffersontown Elementary, two; and Dunn Elementary, two. Interest seems to spring up whenever a Cadre member moves to a new school. Strength in numbers is a reality.

Cadre teachers find strength and solace with other members in their schools, and they gain renewed strength in Cadre gatherings. As mentioned in chapter 2, when the Cadre first began, they met monthly to share and reconnect. As of 2009, the Cadre has had one or two workshops per semester, in addition to a two-week summer institute.

In addition to finding renewal together, teachers have found a new sense of joy through the implementation of the Waldorf-inspired curriculum and pedagogy. Mona Jones mentioned how she had gotten so involved in her early years of teaching that she became overwhelmed and burned out. When her principal, Mike Miller, first approached her about the Cadre, she told him she was not interested:

I was so burned out with running programs early on in my career that I said, "I am not going to do another thing, nothing." I promised myself. And he walked in and said, "This is something you cannot say 'no' to; you cannot." So after I talked to Caroline and found out what it was, it is true—I could not say "no" to it. So I got to go to California for two summers in a row for two weeks, to Rudolf Steiner College, which was, I think, one of the highlights of my life. I began to have more fun.... It was me, everything about it: the eurythmy, everything, the singing, the knitting, the language, the painting, the math lessons, the movement. I just couldn't believe it. And it has probably been what has kept me in education. (personal interview)

Mona had reconnected with her joy for teaching through the arts, as well as through "the art of education." According to Steiner (2007), "In life it is not the ready-made knowledge that has value, but the work that leads to this knowledge, and particularly in the art of education this work has its own special value" (p. 9). In other words, by immersing herself in the process, she was able to revitalize her teaching.

Jan Kovac talked about the fact that her experience with Waldorf gave her increased confidence in her teaching:

> I am walking my way through the curriculum, and it has been really interesting, because I used to get so nervous. And now I walk in and I just know that I am going to have this flow going. I don't worry anymore. (personal interview)

Debbie Lockyear found her experience with Waldorf helped her treat her kids with more respect, ultimately renewing her joy for teaching. In Steiner's (2007) influential book, *Balance in Teaching,* he states: "Reverence, enthusiasm, and a sense of guardianship, these three are actually the panacea, the magic remedy, in the soul of the educator and teacher" (p. 28). Debbie spoke of this:

> It gives groundedness, I think, and an ability to work a little more patiently. I hear teachers screaming in the halls, and there were a couple of days that, being surrounded by that different mentality, I found myself doing it, and I just lost all of my energy. My energy was gone, my happiness at being there; my drive for being there was gone. So I think it really helps me give an example to other people of how to treat kids with more respect. (personal interview)

Shannon Conlon also found that the teachers in her Waldorf-inspired team at Byck helped to influence other members of the school community. One teacher implemented a discipline plan inspired by Waldorf education, and according to Shannon it became a school-wide policy: "There are things that come as a result of the Waldorf-inspired classes that we have pulled over for the whole school" (personal interview).

Being a member of the Waldorf-inspired Cadre has a number of benefits. Not only do teachers receive high-quality art supplies for their classrooms, ongoing professional development, and inspiration through community, they have also been given a renewed sense of self, which has kept many of them in teaching. The work of bringing Waldorf-inspired pedagogy into the public schools, however, is not without challenges.

Challenges, Big and Small

When public-school educators embark on the deeply committed experience of bringing Waldorf-inspired teaching to their students, they do not do this in a vacuum. Unfortunately, such teachers, like most public-school teachers in the U.S., teach in a highly politicized environment, where standards and test scores permeate the culture. Teachers are "not allowed" to bring other curricula to their students, especially in the academic areas of literacy and mathematics. Schools have adopted standards-based literacy and math series with scripted lessons and prefabricated assessments. In the Jefferson County Public Schools, for example, the current reading series was designed specifically for the county to go hand in hand with the standardized achievement tests. Teachers are clearly instructed to teach literacy for a specific amount of time each day. Kelly Cole described her experience with her school reading program and her inability to integrate Waldorf-inspired methods into that subject:

> This year, I have not talked much about it [Waldorf education], mainly because we are a reading-first school. I am new here, walking the line very gently. Our morning is rough, because it leads right into that ninety-minute block [of literacy].... I do not want to mess with that. I don't want to get in trouble, basically, so I just leave it until the afternoon. (personal interview)

Mona also talked about the sacred-cow reading program. She has been reluctant to do a circle in the morning, since teachers are expected to begin their day immediately with reading groups:

They want us to do reading groups first thing in the morning. If I could get away with even a five-or ten-minute circle, just some sort of a routine and a ritual, because the kids love it. (personal interview)

Teachers are actually *scared* to implement what they know is best for children. They are afraid, because principals are continuously pushed to improve test scores to avoid having a "failing school." When this happens—meaning too many of the children did not achieve proficiency on the TEST—it could mean a job loss for a principle. Consequently, Cadre teachers must be very intentional when bringing any Waldorf-inspired curriculum or pedagogy to their students. For some, this has been positive, because it helped teachers connect what they have to teach with what they want to teach. Mona experienced this with one of her principals:

It was a pretty good experience, because I had to explain what I was doing.... [The principal] came in because our test scores did not reflect that we were learning the core content well enough. Anyway, I think she got to know me over the two years, and she could see how I could fit in chalkboard drawings, how I could fit in beeswax-crayon drawings, and how I could fit in painting and the recorder. And she became a little more trusting of me. (personal interview)

Although it is a challenge for teachers to have to prove that Waldorf-inspired methods are good for children, they continually prove that they are up for that challenge. Kelly Cole explained that she had to wait until January of one particular school year to bring storytelling and painting into her class. She felt that she needed to educate her parent body about what she intended to do first, however:

We have parent-teacher conferences in February, and I am going to show them the main-lesson books and the paintings. I will just say, "We are doing this, and here is why we are doing it, and I just wanted to let you know." And talk to them a little bit about the storytelling. I feel like I have my feet on the ground here; I know what I am doing, I know the people are supportive of me here, so I am going to start at least doing this [storytelling] regularly, once a week. I do feel that the parents need to understand why their children are coming home saying whatever they are doing. I have no qualms about saying it to them; I just wasn't ready until now. (personal interview)

Cadre teachers have to feel ready and confident to implement Waldorf-inspired teaching in the classroom. In addition to preparing themselves philosophically, teachers must also have confidence in the methodology or technique. A number of Cadre teachers have wanted to paint with their students but felt intimidated by the painting process and were unsure of their own painting ability. According to Eisner (2002), "Watercolor is an unforgiving medium. By this I mean watercolor does not tolerate indecisiveness well. Mistakes are hard to camouflage." (p. 14). Eisner says that, as one becomes more confident in watercolor technique, one builds intelligence in that domain. As challenging as painting can be, it is certainly something children need. Brenda spoke of the difficulty she had in the process of painting:

It's scary to me. I love watching them do it, but I am watery. I want to be in there when you're painting, but it scares me. [Brenda's team taught with Donna, and Donna led the painting exercises.] The choleric in me wants me to be successful in every single thing I do; I want to be successful. And I am not successful with that, so no, I do not paint. (personal interview)

Kelly's challenge centered on her concerns about whether her painting lesson fit into the curriculum:

It's not really part of what I am supposed to be teaching. You are not supposed to teach them to paint, really. We do teach arts and humanities, but we have an arts and humanities teacher, so, I have to figure out a way to read between the lines there. (personal interview)

Many Cadre members also spoke about time, or the lack thereof, as a primary problem. According to Kelly:

> It is difficult finding the time to make sure that I make it [Waldorf-inspired teaching] happen, because we have all of this other stuff—assessments and all this other stuff that has to get done. So I've decided that I need to *make* time. Every time I make the time it is…worth every minute. (personal interview)

I found the same to be true with Patty Gilderbloom's fifth-grade class. During the second semester of the 2006–2007 school year, Patty invited me into her classroom every other week to paint with her students. Patty felt she needed my experience painting with children, as well as my help in connecting the painting with the core content. It was difficult to find the time to work painting into their busy schedule, but, as Kelly said, every time we painted with the students, it was worth it. Not only did the behavior of Patty's students improve during the regular painting lessons, but many also commented on the fact that painting was one of the few quiet, reflective times they had during their hectic school week. Kessler (2000) writes, "Stepping out of the fray for a moment, students can begin to gain some distance, some perspective on what they feel so they will be less reactive in social situations" (p. 44).

Through all of the challenges that teachers and administrators face in today's era of accountability, there remains hope that things will change and children's best interests will again be first and foremost. Principal Kris Raitzer shares that sentiment:

> In Jefferson County, where it is all about scores, and where…everything revolves around an index…and success is seen only as a number, it's frustrating for them [Cadre teachers]. It is challenging for them, and it is challenging for me, too, because I have to keep the scores up. It is hard to find that balance. Maybe there really is no balance at this point in public education, since everything is so politicized, and because it's just really a simplistic formula instead of the holistic child. We

are in a tough place in education. But the pendulum will swing, and pretty soon we will be back to a much more child-centered approach. (personal interview)

CONCLUSION

Teachers in the Waldorf-inspired Cadre recognized the value of nurturing their inner lives to keep their teaching alive and in some cases retain them in the profession. Many found that their experience with the Cadre community gave them the strength to keep going and infused their teaching with new life. Others found the methods inherent in Waldorf-inspired teaching to be an antidote to their frustration with the system. Still others deepened their understanding of teaching through a more thorough investigation of child development. Through their own renewed joy, teachers were able to bring new inspiration to their students and to a number of their colleagues. Although the implementation of a Waldorf-inspired pedagogy into the public-school setting is not without its problems, nearly all of the Cadre members believe that it is worth the extra effort.

6

LOOKING TOWARD THE FUTURE
WITH HOPE

"Hope is not prognostication. It is an orientation of the spirit, an orientation of the heart; it transcends the world that is immediately experienced, and is anchored somewhere beyond its horizons." (Václav Havel 2004, 82)

IMPLICATIONS AND CONCLUSIONS

As WE MOVE STRIDENTLY through the beginning years of the twenty-first century, educators and those with an interest in education continue to search for schools and schooling that engage and motivate students. During the past thirty years, scholars have published a myriad of books and articles on schools that work. Some focus on true and meaningful education, while others see successful schools as those that reflect the competitive nature of our global culture. Armstrong (2006) believes that the published lists of "best schools" reflect a "disturbing trend in this country" (and across the world) to use test scores and a "rigorous academic curriculum" as the primary criteria for defining what constitutes a "superior learning environment" (p. 2). The present study makes no quantifying claims, but represents a group of teachers engaged in teaching children in unique and meaningful ways. It adds to the body of literature that identifies innovative schools and school programs across the country.

In this final chapter, I discuss necessary ingredients for ongoing professional-development programs and identify several powerful ideas that arose from the study, which might prove relevant to other educators interested in integrating Waldorf-inspired pedagogy into their schools and classrooms. These ideas include the spiritual quality of Waldorf-inspired methods, a strong sense of community among the Cadre teachers, and the ever-present use of the arts. Finally, I include suggestions from the Cadre intended to improve our program and to help others who would like to replicate part or all of this program.

CREATING AND SUSTAINING
MEANINGFUL PROFESSIONAL DEVELOPMENT

Professional-development programs come and go, bringing numerous innovative teaching strategies that may or may not make their way into the day-to-day teaching in public schools. Some programs follow the current trends of educational research and go in and out of fashion as do shoes or clothing. Others are one-shot deals that may offer one or two interesting games or methods, but if no follow-up exists, the methods are easily forgotten. Then there are programs that touch the hearts and souls of teachers and kids. These programs, if properly supported, tend to stay around, grow, and become a natural part of a school and even a school district.

The Waldorf-inspired Project is one such program. Now entering its fifteenth year, the Cadre remains strong and has grown in breadth and depth. Similar in intent to Parker Palmer's "Courage to Teach" now known as the "Teacher Formation Program," the Waldorf-inspired Project continues to offer teachers spiritual support and inner development through ongoing workshops, mentoring, classroom supplies, and scholarships for further training. The Cadre has attracted new members each year, and although a number of teachers have retired, transferred, or moved, membership remains constant, with around thirty teachers actively involved.

In reviewing various Waldorf-inspired initiatives around the country, I have yet to find a program similar to the Cadre project. Several attributes of the project contribute to its uniqueness, including ongoing funding, supportive administration (at both the university and K–12 level), strong and dedicated leadership, and teacher commitment.

Ongoing Funding

Often, when educational programs get off the ground through grants, they end once the money runs out. Many grantors believe programs should become self-sufficient after a given number of years, yet we have been fortunate to receive continued funding from the Norton Foundation. This is due in part to the purpose and mission of the Waldorf-inspired Project, which is synonymous with the Norton Foundation's mission: to support artistic, spiritual, and holistic education. Moreover, because the Waldorf-inspired Project continues to grow and develop, the Norton Foundation believes it is important to help with funding to insure the success and growth of the project. Finally, with support and funding from Bellarmine University, the Norton Foundation knows that it is not the only support for the project. As mentioned, the grant from the Norton Foundation covers scholarships for teachers, purchases high-quality art supplies for Cadre classrooms, brings in guest speakers and artists for workshops, and offers a stipend for the project director.

Administrative Support

Teachers in the Waldorf-inspired Cadre receive support and encouragement from their administrators. For most members, this support was not instantaneous; it had to be earned. Public-school administrators normally know little about Waldorf education. Teachers who wish to use methods inspired by Waldorf education must gain the trust of their principals. In the current climate of accountability and standards, the use of methods other than those intended to improve test scores directly are frequently viewed with trepidation or considered a waste of time. However, trust and support naturally arise when a principal begins to see and understand the quality of community that a Cadre teacher builds in the classroom and that, despite (or *because* of) the methods, students still score above average on their exams. Once they become aware of the quality of education that students receive in a Cadre member's classroom, some principals actually try to fill open positions in their schools with more Cadre members.

Administrative support at the K–12 level is crucial for the success of a professional development program. It is also critical to have such support in higher education. Although the Cadre project began in public schools, it is now housed at the university. The deans, provosts, and university president have consistently supported the project to varying degrees, depending on the political climate of the university. I have received financial support for additional faculty and space, monies for books and supplies, and always moral encouragement. I have not always received recognition of the program's importance, however, which limits its ability to grow and reach a greater regional population. Perhaps this is because I do not know the ins and outs of the political scene and do not have the time to work it out. Eventually I would love to see publicity for our Waldorf-inspired program reach beyond the city limits of Louisville.

Strong Leadership

From its inception, the Waldorf-inspired Cadre has had a strong and dedicated leader. Originally created by Caroline Pinné, the Cadre grew and matured under her tutelage. Caroline knew that if the Cadre were to continue they would need to come together often, offer one another moral and spiritual support, and learn fresh ways to bring Waldorf-inspired education to students in the public-school setting. She did this through workshops, retreats, and opportunities to attend the two-week summer institute at Rudolf Steiner College. Caroline also secured funding for teachers to have quality art supplies and books, which help teachers bring a deeper Waldorf-inspired pedagogy to their students. When the Cadre reached a point where it needed to move to the next level, Caroline sought out another leader and spent an entire year working with me and introducing me to the teachers, administrators, and funders involved in the project.

It was critical for Caroline to choose someone whose passion for Waldorf in the public schools was equal to hers. Some find it uncanny that we met—that Caroline found someone in higher education whose area of research was Waldorf education in the public-school setting. I have always believed that I was led to Louisville to do this work.

Committed Teachers

It is clear that the teachers whose voices fill this book had to be committed to their work with the Waldorf-inspired Cadre. Many were drawn to it, owing to their artistic inclinations and their conviction that students deserved more than the standard fare of today's standards and textbooks. Some saw their colleagues become enchanted again with teaching and wanted that inspiration themselves. Still others recognized immediately that Waldorf-inspired pedagogy would engage and motivate their students. Whatever the reason, those who joined the Cadre were not weak teachers but seekers, looking for the best possible way to form deep and lasting connections with their students that would inevitably lead to a sustained and meaningful education.

As mentioned, a small number of Cadre members have been unable to continue integrating Waldorf-inspired methods into their classrooms. The demands of NCLB caused them to surrender to the more pedantic forms of teaching preferred by most administrators. Others still use Waldorf-inspired methods, but do not attend meetings, workshops, or training; they simply lack the time in their busy lives. Because of these twenty-first-century realities, I admire even more those teachers who remained committed and, despite the difficult demands and mandates, continue to teach in ways that, in their hearts and souls, they know are best for their students.

SPIRITUALITY IN EDUCATION

Twenty-first-century education cannot be effective, and public schools cannot thrive or even survive, until certain conceptual implications rarely discussed in relation to public schools are considered. Spirituality in education has been overshadowed largely by the focus on individual achievement, standards, and accountability, as well as by the appalling effects of NCLB. Nonetheless, a number of courageous educational researchers have written about the potential and tremendous effects of spirituality in education.

Linda Lantieri's (2001) collection, *Schools with Spirit,* calls for a new and bold vision for our schools, "one that reclaims them as soulful places of learning, where the spiritual dimension is welcomed" (xi). She contends that writing about spirituality in education is risky, but by not recognizing the sacred, "our schools run the risk of raising a whole generation of young people who will be bereft of the wisdom and connectedness they need to live a fully human life" (xiv).

The visionary educators who promote soulful teaching are cited throughout this book, including Rachel Kessler, Bill Ayers, Parker Palmer, Angeles Arrrien, and Nel Noddings. Noddings (1992) contends that everyone needs to feel part of something greater than themselves. To me, this something constitutes our individual and collective spirituality. Public schools would be wise to adopt a philosophy and methodology that enhances matters of the spirit.

Throughout this book, I have written of the soul needs of students and teachers, and the way in which Waldorf-inspired teaching tends to meet these needs. From building community to engaging students in deep and meaningful learning to nurturing the inner lives of teachers, their souls and spirits are being fed. Cadre members do not teach spirituality overtly in their classrooms; rather, they include reverence and respect for the natural world, caring and acceptance, and a connectionist worldview as parts of a "spiritual" pedagogy. Such concepts are woven daily into the curriculum and instruction.

Reverence and Respect

Reverence and respect for the natural world is emphasized in a number of ways in Cadre teachers' classrooms. Teachers begin their mornings with a verse. Not all use the same one, but this is an example that many have adopted:

> May my feet rest firmly on the ground
> May my head touch the sky
> May I see clearly
> May I have the capacity to listen
> May I be free to touch
> May my words be true
> May my heart and mind be open
> May my hands be empty to fill the need
> May my arms be open to others
> May my gifts be revealed to me
> So I may return that which has been given
> Completing the great circle.
>
> (The Terma Collective)

The use of this morning verse and others like it is an effective way to begin the day, reminding children to be thankful for what they have, who they are, and how they can help one another.

The units of study on ecology and the environment emphasize respect and reverence for the natural world. For example, Jo Anne Noland, a kindergarten teacher at Gilmore Lane, created a classroom garden with her students. Rather than study plants from a book or a computer, her children can experience the beauty of living plants that they have planted and tend. The awe and wonder on their faces when the first bulb pokes its leaves out of the ground in spring is priceless. The idea of school gardens is not unique, yet it is still the exception more than the rule.

Another Cadre member was required to teach about the basic needs of plants. The teacher's guide suggested that children plant seeds and use one plant for the control and two other plants as the experiment. The control would receive sunlight and water, whereas one plant would not be watered and the other would not receive light. Essentially, this classic experiment, which denies a fine seed the opportunity to grow into a healthy plant, teaches children that plants are expendable. Because this Cadre member was attuned to the wonders of the natural world and did not want to teach disrespect for nature, she changed the experiment to see what could be *added* to the experimental plants to *enhance* their growth. This is a powerful yet simple idea. Imagine what would happen if all science curricula across the country would incorporate such changes.

These are only a few examples of how Cadre members integrate the teaching of reverence and respect into their curricula, but they give a sense of the inclusive nature in their teaching styles. Not only do Cadre members teach reverence and respect for the natural world; they also seamlessly weave respect for self and for one another through an emphasis on caring and acceptance in their classrooms.

Caring and Acceptance

Another aspect of spiritual pedagogy involves acceptance and care. Most elementary teachers are caring people by nature; they become elementary educators because they love and care for children. Cadre members incorporate certain Waldorf-inspired methods into their classrooms that enhance their relationships with the children. The initial handshake at the start of the day tends to get most children off to a good start. It is a focused gesture that helps students know they are accepted, and that their teachers are happy to see them. The teachers' use of musical transitions (through singing or chimes) between subjects sets the mood for a peaceful and accepting classroom culture. In elementary-school classrooms, teachers often have to raise their voices during a transition, which the children can experience as harsh and unwelcoming.

In addition to these ways that Cadre teachers embed caring and acceptance naturally into classrooms, teachers subtly give students the message that they are worth the extra effort by the very act of going beyond state-mandated core content and offering lessons filled with innovative and engaging subject matter.

Interestingly, Cadre teachers' classroom décor suggests an ethic of care for their students. Many elementary-school classrooms are downright ugly, with ready-made pictures and posters all over the walls, various items hanging from the ceiling, and every available nook and cranny stuffed with material. Although teachers in the Cadre cannot keep their classrooms as spare as a typical Waldorf private school classroom, they nevertheless add aesthetic touches wherever possible. Most Cadre teachers use hand-dyed silks to soften the environment. They incorporate nature in beautiful, hands-on nature tables, use lamps for low-level lighting, and paint their white boards with black chalkboard paint so that they can offer their students lively chalk drawings. Students appreciate their teachers' efforts. One student commented to Donna Stottman: "You really like nature, don't you Ms. Stottman? You always have something from nature in our classroom."

Connectionist Perspective

Throughout my work with Waldorf education and Cadre members, I have found that they approach teaching with a connectionist perspective. Goodman (1992) contends that a connectionist perspective,

> places one's connection to the lives of all human beings and other living things on our planet at the center of the educational process.... The radical reforming of our schools needs to be centered on helping children understand the ways in which life on this planet is interconnected and interdependent and that in caring for others we are caring for ourselves. (p. 28)

I have also found that Cadre members use what I term "connective pedagogy" (Goral 2000): "Connective pedagogy takes into consideration a deep, lasting relationship between teacher and student and a curriculum that connects and integrates all subject areas" (p. 54). Teachers in the Waldorf-inspired Cadre do not stay with their students for the ideal eight years as private Waldorf-school teachers do, but many of them loop with their students and are able to build strong bonds in the two years they have together. Despite the fact that teachers are bound by law to the state core content, Cadre teachers nevertheless do their best to integrate literature, movement, and the arts into their academic subjects.

Goodman asserts that "an elementary curriculum that fosters a connectionist perspective reflects a radical departure from the status quo" (p. 124). This statement rings true for me in my work with the Cadre. Their approach to teaching and their use of Waldorf-inspired methods is certainly a departure from those used by most of their colleagues. Because these teachers work in a public-school setting, they do not overtly teach spirituality to their students; but their approach nurtures each child's soul and spirit, and this makes their teaching stand apart from those who merely attend to their students' intellects.

THE CADRE COMMUNITY

Another aspect that contributes to the ongoing success of the Waldorf-inspired Cadre is community. As defined by Wolf (1996), community is "a group of people who come together for a common purpose in a spirit of helpfulness and harmony" (p. 51). Jung (1973) believed the longing of humans to have a connection to one another is universal, and Steiner (1994) held that, if we fail to develop within our beings a very strong sense that there is something beyond ourselves, we will be unable to find the strength to evolve to something higher. This longing for community and desire to work for a higher purpose continually brings the Cadre together. As discussed in chapter 2, the Cadre meets regularly for various purposes. In the early years, Cadre teachers met monthly for support and professional development. As the project grew and changed, and as expectations from the district increased, meetings became fewer, though they are just as powerful and necessary. We also provide ongoing classes, in which a number of Cadre members enroll to learn more about Waldorf-inspired pedagogy and Steiner's philosophy. In this community of teachers, I have found three very important traits that echo the research on community building in organizations: shared values, self-sustaining community resources, and a reduction of outside resources that maintain the status quo (Comer 1996; Goodman 1992).

Shared Values

According to Comer (1996), "in every interaction, you are either building community or breaking community" (p. 148). In my work with the Waldorf-inspired Cadre, I found their commitment to building community quite strong, mostly because of their shared belief in the value of Waldorf-inspired education for their students. Because these

teachers have self-selected to be a part of the particular educational initiative, they want to do this work and have agreed to balance their individuality by an ethos of community. Goodman (1992) believes, "When
the value of either individuality or community significantly supersedes
the other, then the one which dominates distorts the democratic ideal"
(p. 10). Teachers still active in the Cadre seem to have retained this balance successfully, maintaining a healthy community.

In addition to the shared common belief that using Waldorf-inspired
methods are the best way to teach children, teachers also share other
values. Most have a strong artistic sense and an inner knowing that the
arts must be integrated into their core curriculum. Not only do they
value the arts, but they are also artistically talented. Some Cadre members are excellent vocalists, others are instrumentalists. A number of
the Cadre excel at handwork and use their talents with their students.
Others can draw and/or paint. Still others are kinesthetically gifted
and regularly bring movement to the children. It is interesting that
most Cadre members had already used the arts with students before
discovering Waldorf education.

Another shared value is that of maintaining a creative, child-centered classroom environment. Rather than succumb to the ethos of
many public schools, Cadre teachers must teach creatively, imbuing
their methodology with as many Waldorf-inspired practices as possible. As a number of Cadre members mentioned in the previous chapter,
learning and integrating Waldorf-inspired pedagogy into their teaching kept them in the teaching profession. The deadening practice of
today's scripted curricula is rarely found in these teachers' classrooms.
This does not mean that Cadre teachers do not use the core content,
but that they know how to make the core content come alive.

Cadre members also value the developmentally appropriate practices of Waldorf education. They share an understanding of the
importance of child-centered teaching, which allows them to recog-
nize the critical significance of teaching content at a developmentally
appropriate time. Through the many classes and workshops, teachers
have learned countless methods to meet their children where they are.
For example, Donna Stottman was required to teach her beginning

fourth-grade students how to use a compass. She began by telling them a story about a young boy who was sitting up in a tree watching a donkey that was tied to a post. As he gazed at the animal, he noticed that the donkey was tramping a perfect circle in the grass while going round and round the post. Donna described how ancient mathematicians developed the compass by using a string and a stationary post. The children then made their own compasses, and finally she introduced the modern-day tool to the eagerly awaiting fourth-graders. How different this approach is from whisking a compass out of a plastic bin and plopping it down in front of the students, complete with a worksheet for practice.

Cadre teachers value the caring and compassionate methods advocated by most holistic educators. Ron Miller (1999) suggested that, to teach holistically, educators must meet their students with an open-hearted responsiveness, and that this is at the center of holistic education. Frequently in today's schools, caring and teaching students to care is not seen as sufficiently rigorous and is "considered a 'touchy-feely hindrance' to preparing workers who can win the game of global competition" (Wolk 2007, 653). Yet Cadre members intuitively understand the necessity of valuing each and every student and preserving their dignity with caring methods and practices.

The values shared by Cadre teachers add to their sense of community. Knowing that they can come together, swap stories, and feel supported and accepted helps them remain idealistic yet committed to the struggle. Eduardo Galeano (2006) refers to this as "rebellious imagination":

> Capitulatory imagination seeks escape from responsibility. Rebellious imagination embraces it, enlarges it, celebrates it. It lets us view the world with fresh eyes. Sometimes, it makes possible an unlikely transformation by restoring us to a new kind of innocence, one in which experience, no matter how dismal, is subsumed within a larger, more luminous vision: the gleam in the eye of those who have every reason to weep. (p. 128)

Yet another reason to keep a "gleam in the eye" is the *self-sustaining* aspect of community.

Self-sustaining Community

In their research on establishing School Development Programs (Comer Process for Reforming Education), Emmons, Comer, and Haynes (1996) found that, when changing social structures, the emphasis must be placed on building local expertise and capacity. By involving the stakeholders, the community is self-sustaining and can thus survive and even thrive. Although initial training for Cadre members took place at Rudolf Steiner College, professional development at the local level began almost immediately.

Chapter 2 goes into detail on the many staff-development workshops that Cadre members presented to other teachers, as well as to their own group. Research on successful professional development also indicates that training those who are part of your organization helps sustain programs. Owing to financial constraints, time, and distance, it is not always possible to bring in outside experts. When given the opportunity to train other teachers, Cadre members felt honored and trusted, thus committing to the community at an even deeper level.

As mentioned, early in the Cadre history, the group met monthly, when various members would lead their colleagues in various artistic activities. They would also share stories of successful implementation of Waldorf-inspired pedagogy in their classes, along with examples of students' work. This became more formalized through the years and has come to be called the Cadre showcase. Once each year, Cadre members present activities they have implemented in their classes in order to share their experiences with other Cadre teachers and invited guests.

Our summer institute also makes use of local Cadre members. In summer 2007, Mona Jones taught recorder and Donna Stottman shared the content of our Language Arts course. Moreover, we take advantage of the talented teachers from our own Waldorf school, who are honorary members of the Cadre. Our summer institute and many workshops offered throughout the year involve teachers from the Waldorf School of Louisville. In addition to using local resources in the form of Cadre teachers, I deliver many workshops and classes.

However, I try to limit my teaching, as I believe it is important for students to gain information from a variety of personalities.

Steering Clear of the Status Quo

Many educators in our country follow the path of least resistance. It is not for me to say, however, whether this is because of a fear of authority, standing out, or just plain fatigue from the struggle. I do know that going along with the crowd in this particular standards-based age of accountability is *not* the best we can do for our children or teachers. Strength requires courage and community. In his essay "The Flight of Our Dreams," Galeano (2006) writes about the importance of courage and standing up for what is right. He shares the words of women's suffrage pioneer, Susan B. Anthony:

> Anthony challenged the debilitating effect of timidity when she wrote that "cautious, careful people, always casting about to preserve their reputation and social standing, never can bring about a reform. Those who are really in earnest must be willing to be anything or nothing in the world's estimation." Anthony challenges us to pursue our convictions without hesitation and, equally important, without concern for appearances or decorum. (p. 131)

Educators interested in making significant change cannot be afraid to stand out, nor can they be timid in their efforts to make a difference. Cadre members find strength in numbers. How easy it would be to join the status quo, to read from the script, to put the kids in rows and turn to page 68 to copy twenty sentences. Yet they persevere, sometimes against great odds. Teachers in the Waldorf-inspired Cadre seem to avoid status quo in a number of ways, including working together in the same school, attending professional development sessions, and taking classes to further their education.

Working Together

Teachers in the Cadre are routinely challenged in regard to their implementation of Waldorf-inspired methods. Other teachers have made deragotory comments such as: "Oh, that's the Waldorf stuff, where you just dance around in a circle all day." If Cadre teachers have support in their own building (they try to teach in the same buildings together when possible), it becomes much easier to deflect negative comments. In situations where Cadre teachers have formed teams—such as the Dixie Elementary team (1998–2002) and the ongoing team at Byck Elementary—they are able to provide workshops for the other teachers in their building and offer performance days, when they showcase their students' work.

When Patty Rundell, Jennifer Geroski, Tina Marsteller, and Barbara Doyle taught together at Dixie Elementary, they were able to do some pretty remarkable work. Patty was the pioneer for Waldorf-inspired pedagogy at Dixie and, through her efforts, inspired the three other teachers to join her.

Byck Elementary organized their team in 1994, when Mary Holden, an original Cadre member, taught there. Along with Melanie Holiday and their principal Sharon Shrout, Mary decided to form a Waldorf-inspired team (see brochure on following pages). They recruited a teacher for each grade level, K–5. All teachers went to the Rudolf Steiner College public-school institute, and during the early years the team would come together regularly for various activities. One such event was a Friday afternoon arts-and-humanities time. Each teacher chose an area of expertise, such as knitting, recorder playing, or painting, and children from grades K–5 would sign up for a particular class. In this way students got to meet other teachers on the team, team members had the experience of teaching to their strength and passion, and they built community through this shared effort.

More recently, students of teachers on the Byck team perform for their schoolmates, strengthening their community through this ritual. Just as students in private Waldorf schools perform regularly for festivals and holidays, these students do the same, although they often choose different holidays on which to perform. For example, over the past few years Byck students perform during Black History Month. Students recite poems by Langston Hughes, sing spirituals, and perform modern-day raps. According to Williams, Oberman, and Goral

(2008), Waldorf methods are now being tested in difficult urban areas as a means to address the staggering problems of poor student achievement. These methods are connected to student engagement in learning and teachers who have the tools and techniques to inspire students.

These rituals are a powerful means to form community. Rituals bring people together in a deeper, more intentional way than other types of gatherings—perhaps because the very nature of rituals is to bring heart and meaning to those involved. School-based rituals are critically important in sustaining teachers' work community. The ritual of gathering for workshops with the Cadre is also important.

Cadre Professional Development

Teachers have many opportunities to attend staff-development sessions through their schools and through the district. JCPS employees are required to attend twenty-four hours of professional development each year. Many Cadre teachers fulfill the hours through mandatory professional development sessions, yet still choose to attend Cadre meetings, where they receive additional hours of professional development. Cadre teachers choose to come to these sessions not because they need the hours, but because they need the community and the offerings are very different from the required status quo. As mentioned in chapter 2, Cadre sessions resemble family reunions. Teachers are so happy to see one another and be together with like-minded colleagues. As one Cadre member stated, "These meetings are like a breath of fresh air" (personal interview). Other teachers have shared that the professional development sessions rejuvenate them and inspire them to continue implementing Waldorf-inspired methods into their classrooms.

Our sessions are far from the typical mainstream workshops for professional development. They focus on the academic curriculum, but themes are routinely integrated or highlight the arts. At the fall 2008 workshop, for example, Betty Staley presented a Friday-evening lecture and an all-day Saturday workshop on teaching history and multicultural education through the arts. She used storytelling, drama, music, art, and poetry during the two days. A Cadre member had this to say about the workshop:

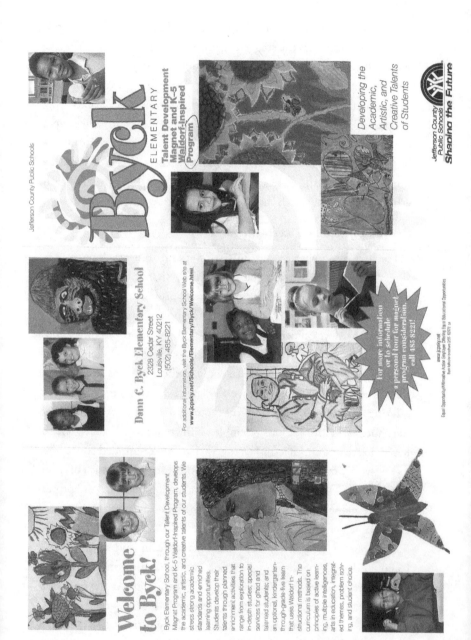

Byck Elementary brochure about teaching

Talented and Gifted (TAG) Services

- Commonwealth-Certified TAG Resource Teacher and TAG Lab
- Individual Service Plans
- Curriculum Differentiation
- Cluster Grouping of TAG Students
- Flexible Grouping Across Grades

The DISCOVER Assessment

Byck uses the DISCOVER Assessment and Cognitive Abilities testing to identify students in kindergarten through grade five for TAG services. Students test for the JCPS District Advance Program in grades three, four, and five. Byck is a designated JCPS Advance Program site.

Why do we attempt to identify potentially gifted students at an early age and to provide services to meet their unique needs? First, research indicates that it is important to stimulate a child's brain at an early age. Second, gifted children who experience frustration and boredom in the Primary grades may "go underground" in the Intermediate grades.

DISCOVER is a performance-based test that measures students' problem-solving abilities. It requires the use of spatial, logical, mathematical, linguistic, and interpersonal skills. The problems and challenges that students work on range from those requiring convergent thinking to those needing unique solutions and divergent thought.

Byck ELEMENTARY

K–5 Waldorf Inspired Methods Team

Students have the option of placement on this unique team that uses aspects of Waldorf methodology.

Academic subjects are balanced with rich artistic experiences and demanding practical work to challenge students to reach their full potential. Rhythm, song, color, dance, handwork, painting, poetry, storytelling, and drama are woven into the curriculum and are made part of all subjects at all grade levels.

The Waldorf Methods Team is available to students in kindergarten through grade five. The teachers have participated in the Rudolf Steiner College Public School Institute in California and are members of the Jefferson County Public Schools (JCPS) Cadre.

Talent Development Magnet Enrichment

Students identify and develop their academic, artistic, and creative talents through a unique curriculum that includes awareness activities, enrichment learning, in-depth studies, and additional support services for exceptionally talented students.

- **Day Trips:** Students become aware of the many opportunities available to them through extensive exposure to museums, theaters, historical sites, nature centers, and other community resources.
- **Workshops and Special Areas:** Students explore their interests in special areas, such as media and technology, visual and performing arts, and foreign language. They further investigate their interests through workshops held by such organizations as Kentucky Museum of Art and Craft, Walden Theatre, Young Playwrights, U of L Repertory Theatre, and the Louisville Orchestra.
- **In-Depth Studies:** Students develop their talents during grades four and five through in-depth studies of such areas as architecture, journalism, broadcasting, theatre arts, performing arts and humanities groups, and media/communications.

in the Waldorf-inspired methods team

There are times in your life when your spirit remembers things of the past and future, even as you sit on this physical plane inhabiting a physical body. The experience of sharing with Betty Staley was not of this physical world for me. I was able to rise above and beyond my physical limitations and allow my spirit to soar. There was so much learned, remembered, and experienced, that human words cannot express. (Carolyn Hamilton 2007)

Traditional Classes with Nontraditional Themes

Although we offer classes at Bellarmine for both Master's credit and non-credit options, our class topics are not for closed minds and those afraid to step out of the box. Our Waldorf-inspired courses (offered during the two-week institute in the summer and during the fall and spring semesters) offer something unique to our students. For example, the summer 2008 course on child development taught Steiner's theory of the development of the human being, comparing and contrasting this with traditional theories of child development. Our second class, Teaching Science through the Arts, focused on the Waldorf science curriculum and developmentally appropriate ways to teach science in grades one through eight.

We begin each morning with eurythmy or singing classes. Teachers who attend the two-week summer institute form strong bonds and connections with one another. Over the past three summers, I have received comments from students about the community formed during the two weeks together: "I could not have asked for anything to have been different or improved. This has been a fabulous, life-changing two weeks!" "Awesome is an understatement. [This institute] has been life-changing for so many people. The experience radiates far beyond this class." "The institute was very nourishing. I cannot wait until next summer."

Unfortunately, some Cadre members have been unable to avoid the status quo in recent years. District requirements are so time consuming and taxing that teachers have little time or energy for offering Waldorf-inspired methods to the children. It requires a monumental effort and strong community support to go against the status quo.

I am not in the trenches of the public schools, working, as Bill Ayers (2004) says, in this tension,

> one foot planted in the mud and muck of the world as we find it, the other striving toward a world that could be. We toil in fields not entirely of our making; we plant seeds for harvests we can only begin to imagine. (p. 144)

Yet it is my sincere hope that all those who know of and have implemented Waldorf-inspired techniques with their students will somehow find their way back to this. As Victoria Stafford (2006), in her brilliant essay "The Small Work in the Great Work," states:

> Our mission is to plant ourselves at the gates of Hope—not the prudent gates of Optimism, which are somewhat narrower; nor the stalwart, boring gates of Common Sense; nor the strident gates of Self-Righteousness, which creak on shrill and angry hinges (people cannot hear us there; they cannot pass through); nor the cheerful, flimsy garden gate of "Everything is gonna be all right." (p. 188)

Our mission is to continue to see the world "as it is and as it could be; the place from which you glimpse not only struggle, but joy in the struggle" (Stafford 2006, 188).

INSPIRING OUR STUDENTS AND OURSELVES THROUGH THE ARTS

Through more than twenty-five years in education, I have found the arts to be both powerfully motivating and equalizing. Children (and adults) find meaning through the arts, and, perhaps more important, for many children, the arts become their gateway into other subjects. According to Jensen (2000), the arts are central to learning: "The systems they nourish (which include our integrated sensory, attentional, cognitive, emotional, and motor-capacity processes) are in fact the driving force behind all other learning" (p. 3). Consequently, it is difficult to understand why the arts are frequently the first to go when schools cut budgets. During my early years in the public schools, I often found that the children who performed below grade level in traditional academic subjects were my most creative and artistic students. Conte (2001) concurs in her inspiring essay, "The Gift of the Arts":

> For many of the children with whom I have struggled, taught, and learned, the gift of the arts has sometimes meant the difference between safety and violence, emotional clarity or disturbance, school success or failure, belonging or isolation, hope or despair. (p. 78)

Conte states that she continues "to be awed by the power of the arts to nurture human beings and provide transformational, community enhancing experiences" (p. 78). When visiting Cadre member classrooms and speaking with the teachers, their experience of integrating the arts parallels Conte's. Throughout this study, I found that the arts bring students together as a community, help them academically, and assisted in developing young people's "humanness."

The Arts as Community Builder

Recently, I sat in on Laura Wasz's morning circle. The children sang enthusiastically, recited poetry, and participated in simple folk dances at the start of their day. The feeling in her room was one of warmth, meaning, and acceptance. Gardner's (1993) work on multiple intelligences suggests that everyone learns differently and that teachers must offer learning opportunities other than through traditional lectures and rote learning. Many students learn best through art, drama, music, and movement. Laura's teaching incorporated each, both in her morning circle and throughout her day. An example is Laura's unit on Thanksgiving. During a three-day period, children performed a play; cooked and ate a meal; studied, reflected, and wrote about pilgrims and Native Americans; and engaged in a number of visual arts. Laura shared her experience in her final paper for our class, "Teaching History and Multicultural Education in the Waldorf School":

I teach the Pilgrim story every year and this year, as a student of Rudolf Steiner's Waldorf education, I tried specifically to integrate Waldorf methods.... I have always agreed with the wisdom of Steiner's (2000) admonition to "permeate all our teaching with an element of art" (p. 107). So it is with art, drama, and food that I connect information, cross referenced from many books, to take the children on a three-day Pilgrim experience.... As I sang a blessing before our feast of self-made Pilgrim food, I looked out over the sincerely bowed heads of my class and thought how, through this lesson, rich with Waldorf methods, they'd had the opportunity to experience the wonder, gratitude, and responsibility so essential to Waldorf education.

Laura's classroom was not the only one in which I witnessed the community-building power of the arts. As mentioned in chapter 3, nearly all Cadre teachers use the morning circle to begin the day, which inevitably helps build classroom community. Students come together as a group, and each individual's efforts—whether adding a voice to a song, performing the correct movement in a dance, or reciting the right words of a poem—add to the whole. When one person is out of sync, the entire circle is thrown off. Both teachers and students recognized the importance of participating in the circle.

I witnessed another aspect of using the arts to build community while visiting Donna Stottman's fifth-grade classroom. Students had recently completed a painting of pumpkins, and Donna had the paintings laid out for everyone to see. Students were asked to make comments on one another's work. One student might choose a painting with the brightest colors. Donna would ask, "Whose painting is this?" Then a child might point out a painting with the best-formed pumpkin. The process would continue until most of the paintings had been recognized.

Such methods as including and honoring everyone's artwork, as well as the morning circle and many other artistic activities, help build classroom community.

The Arts and Academics

According to Eric Jensen's (1998) research on the arts and academics, arts education enhances creativity, assists general intellectual achievement, facilitates language development, and boosts reading readiness. Research on schools that employ an arts-based philosophy continually show that children in these schools outperform their peers. Jensen reports, "Three countries near the top in rankings of math and science scores (Japan, Hungary, and the Netherlands) all have intensive music and art training built into their elementary school curriculum" (p. 87). In Jensen's book *Arts with the Brain in Mind* (2000), he states, "There is plenty of evidence that engaging students in the arts can and does reach special populations" (p. 64). Petrash (2002) wrote, "I have seen how artistic activities help children to become emotionally engaged in the learning process.... Drawing, singing, painting, and poetry have their regular place in the [Waldorf] educational program" (pp. 59–60).

During a visit to Jo Anne Noland's kindergarten class, I saw how she introduces the letter *K*. She had integrated Waldorf-inspired methods into the program of studies required by JCPS. She began by putting on a story apron and sang a story song. As the song began, the children became quiet:

> Listening listening quietly, listening now and you will see
> Heroes and horses, princes and kings
> Beautiful queens and many fine things
> Listening, listening quietly.

The story for the letter *K* was about an African King named Kuzulu Kalonga. Despite several interruptions, most of the kids were attentive. The story included a song for each task the suitor had to perform. Jo Anne had a thorned stick to represent the thorny trees in the forest, which helped maintain the children's attention. The story ended with these words. "My story goes in, my story goes out. Breathe in, breathe out." The students then returned to their seats, and they sang a song as Jo Anne distributed beeswax crayons:

Crayons are a gift from bees,
Paper is a gift from trees.
Use them with loving care,
They are ours to love and share.

As Jo Anne passed out their new block crayons, the children oohed and ahed. Jo Anne had them use an "alligator grip" on their crayons and explained how to hold the crayons by defining the largest side of the crayon as the "papa bear side," the medium side of the crayon as the "mama bear side," and the smallest side of the crayon as the "baby bear side."

Next, Jo Anne led the children through a guided drawing. Her instructions were as follows: "Draw a circle with yellow for the head, then a rectangle for the neck, then form a small triangle for the dress." After the students finished their drawings, she instructed them to stand up tall and make their arms like the letter *K*. They then painted Ks on painting boards with water and a paint brush. Next, they used colored pencils to make *K*s.

I heard kids saying "down, in, out" as they were drawing/writing the letters. Finally, Jo Anne had the children go around the room and look at one another's work in a circle while holding hands. (field observation)

If we were to analyze the lesson through the lens of Gardner's (1983) multiple intelligences, we would say that Jo Anne managed to incorporate all of them. If we look at the lesson through Jensen's (2000) research on the positive effects of integrating the arts into academic subjects, we would see that, by using the arts, she was able to enhance creativity, assist general intellectual achievement, facilitate language development, and boost reading readiness.

Jo Anne is not the only Cadre member to enhance academics through the integration of the arts. As mentioned, Laura Wasz used drama, visual arts, music, movement and poetry to teach her unit on Thanksgiving. To review what her children had learned, Laura asked them to do two things. First, she had them make a four-section drawing for the covers of their folders labeled "The Voyage," "The Long

Winter," "Spring/Summer," and "Thanksgiving." Laura explained that, in a Waldorf classroom, this drawing would have most likely gone into the children's main-lesson books. For her purposes, however, she wanted to assess the children's understanding of these periods in the pilgrim experience, and she felt that drawing often works better than words in assessing children's understanding. She also had students draw themselves telling someone else about the Pilgrims, using subtext to show their thoughts. Again, Laura blended Waldorf-inspired pedagogy with JCPS core content.

Integrating the arts into the academic subjects is effective. Not only are students more engaged, but they also retain the material, are happier while doing it, and learn to love learning for the sake of learning.

Art as an Expression of Humanness

According to Jensen (2000), the cognitive benefits of the arts are very significant, yet often their nonacademic benefits are under-appreciated. Jensen reports that the arts are known to "support relaxation, creativity, self-discipline, and motivation" (p. 3). Jack Petrash (2002) refers to the arts as a medium to restore balance in schools. He states that, when students are artistically engaged, they can experience healing and positive change. He asserts that the arts help students find direction in life. For younger students, the arts round out their education; for older ones, the arts are often transformative in a student's educational experience: "It is only through a well-balanced approach to teaching that we can help students realize all that they can do and help them to become adults who can realize their full human potential" (Petrash 2002, 101).

Conte (2001) suggests that "the arts play a meaningful role in social and emotional learning and health. Creative-arts experiences often provide expressive opportunities that give voice to emotional material that may be inaccessible through words" (p. 80). Cadre members told me repeatedly of how the arts helped particular students with emotional or social issues. Brenda Chelliah spoke of a young boy who "wasn't making it." As mentioned in chapter 3, Brenda taught across the hall from Donna Stottman. She saw how Donna was able to reach her children through Waldorf-inspired activities. Thus, she began to implement movement, singing, and poetry into her classroom. These arts-based activities helped calm and engage this young student:

> If I couldn't get him to do anything else, I could always get him to do beanbag activities. He had a very behavior-disordered problem, but he would do anything to play a beanbag game. [Sometimes] he would come out of a corner after throwing his desk around the floor. If it was circle time—if we were going to use the wooden rhythm sticks, the copper rods, or pass the beanbag—he wanted to participate. (personal interview)

Other teachers spoke of how their use of Waldorf-inspired methods led their colleagues to believe that they had "gotten the best students." In other words, colleagues actually thought the children in Cadre members' classrooms were smarter and better behaved, whereas students in Cadre teachers' classes were in fact engaged and learning because of their implementation of an arts-infused curriculum.

According to Conte (2001) "Holding the arts central to education is an important part of nurturing people's inner lives" (p. 89). To put it in a different context, by withholding the arts, Fowler (1996) found: "My observations in schools are that drugs, crime, indifference, and insensitivity tend to run rampant in schools that deprive students of instruction in the arts" (pp. 12–13). With such stories supporting the use of the arts, it is difficult to understand why the arts are not a vital part of every school curriculum.

CLOSING COMMENTS

The significant ideas and practices discussed in chapter 6—a highly supportive and well-organized professional development model that focuses on an integration of the arts, a strong community, and education infused with spirit—are powerful concepts and practices that make the Waldorf-inspired Cadre's work effective. Such ideas and practices can enhance the education of children in many public-school settings.

Two key components of the Cadre's success are its continued funding from the Norton Foundation and the guidance of a committed leader.

Sincere and dedicated teachers anywhere can find such funding and leadership. What seems to be more difficult to find is commitment to a type of education that teaches the whole child, one that is respectful and reverent toward nature and to one another, and one that nurtures the inner lives of both students and teachers. Anita Roddick, founder of the Body Shop contends:

> We've got to have an education that measures the morality of our behavior. We've got to have politicians who ask "Is this the right thing to do?" We've got to have media that have a sense of social responsibility and are not all sex and violence, but thoughtful, dissenting, and educating with information. I believe we should be setting up experiential and educational projects in which we talk about the production of shaping the human spirit, rather than polishing people for a job. (1998, 219)

Roddick's moving essay, "Social Responsibility and Business," could offer a model for education as well. It is time for education to become less identified with the mind and more attuned to the spirit.

Steven Wolk (2007) concurs and suggests we need "schooling for human beings" (p. 657):

> We can no longer tinker with a broken and inhuman para-digm of schooling. We must stop schooling our children as if they were products and reclaim our schools as sacred places for human beings. We must rethink our classrooms as vibrant spaces that awaken consciousness to the world, open minds to the problems of our human condition, inspire wonder, and help people to lead personally fulfilling lives. (p. 658)

Indeed, our work as educators and community members is clear, and it is critical that we do not waste more time. By modeling successful programs already in existence, such as the Waldorf-inspired Cadre, students and teachers will be well-served and prepared to lead others in our world to be compassionate rather than competitive, happy and healthy rather than greedy, and giving rather than self-seeking.

As I write these final words, the Waldorf-inspired Cadre Project continues to thrive despite the political climate of NCLB in which we currently live and teach. Long-time educators know that mandates—whether "good" or "bad" for students—ebb and flow. Luckily, our project has survived what I believe to be the worst years in recent history for educators and students.

Through the Cadre teachers' hard work and commitment to what they know is best for children, students are afforded an engaging curriculum that goes beyond best practice, a deep understanding of academic concepts, and a love for school. Teachers build and create strong classroom communities in which they foster a republic of many voices to speak their truths, all within a controlled freedom. Through the Cadre teachers' deep understanding of child development and their integration of Waldorf-inspired methods, including the morning greeting, circle time, and a kinder, gentler approach to classroom management, these communities provide safe havens for our children. Finally, some Cadre teachers have remained in teaching only because of their involvement in the methods inspired by Rudolf Steiner and the strong support of the Cadre community. This community has provided an encouraging context for life-long learning, a deepened understanding of pedagogical excellence, and a renewal of joy in teaching.

We live in precarious times, in a world of unstable climate, rampant greed, and (in our country at least) a public-school education that is often undervalued, taken for granted, and disrespected. Yet despite the odds, hope remains among these teachers and those who support them; what they are doing *is* making a difference in children's lives.

I often tell the Cadre teachers to imagine the twenty-five children they teach each year and how those twenty-five students (multiplied by the number of classes they teach) will take the goodness, the joy, and the beauty gifted to them from their teachers into the world and spread it to even more people. What these teachers are doing is no small task. They balance the heavy demands of an urban school district with their innate love of teaching and their unequivocal knowledge that what they bring to children is absolutely the best, most heartfelt, and love-filled blessing they can give to the world.

APPENDICES

APPENDIX 1: A FRACTION STORY

ONCE UPON A TIME in the land of Snoitcarf, there lived twin princesses. Both girls were blessed with many wonderful qualities. They were smart (especially good in math), clever, and strong. Both had beautiful long, wavy hair that glistened in the sun and sparkling eyes that told stories of their lives. However, the girls were different in noticeable ways. Anna was soft-spoken, kind, generous, dreamy, and loved nature. Anita was quick witted, organized, articulate, and focused. As the girls grew up, these qualities became more and more prevalent.

Now it came to pass, that their mother, Queen Arithma, was getting older and was ready to pass her crown on to one of her daughters. She knew her daughters well and was acutely aware of their strengths as well as their weaknesses. Anita would be an excellent ruler—direct, efficient, good with money—but would she be kind and compassionate with the people of Snoitcarf? Anna, on the other hand, might not run the country in an organized manner. She was so dreamy—yet her kindness and generosity with the people was unquestionable. Queen Arithma thought and thought about who would make the best queen. She was supposed to make her decision soon at a large gathering of the people of Snoitcarf. And so she devised a plan...

One day while Anita was sitting in the garden, seriously contemplating what horse she would ride that day, an old woman approached her. The old woman was a crone—she wore a black cloak with a hood, had a craggy face and a big nose with a wart on it. She approached Anita and said "Excuse me, young lady, but I have a question for you." Anita looked up with surprise.

"What do you want old woman?"

The old crone replied. "I am from a neighboring country. We have had some hard times. We do not have enough food to feed our people. I was wondering if some of our people could move to Snoitcarf and perhaps live in the southern half of your country."

Anita answered quickly. "I don't think that would be possible. We don't have enough land and that is where our horses run freely. No, I don't think so. Please be gone."

And the old woman left with these words, "As you wish."

That very same day, Anna was walking along the river bank, looking at the sky and the beautiful clouds overhead. Lost in thought, she was startled when someone tapped her on the back. Interestingly, it was the same old woman. She wore the same black cloak, with the same hood, her face was craggy and she had a big nose with a wart on it. Even more interesting, is the fact that she asked Anna the same question. "Excuse me young lady, but I have a question for you." Anna came out of her dream world with a start.

"Oh my, you startled me. Whatever do you want?"

The old crone replied. "I am from a neighboring country. We have had some hard times. We do not have enough food to feed our people. I was wondering if some of our people could move to Snoitcarf and perhaps live in the southern half of your country."

"Well, that is a good question," answered Anna. "Perhaps it would work. Maybe your people could live and work with some of our people and learn our customs. But I cannot make that decision on my own. I must ask my mother, the queen."

And the old woman left with these words, "As you wish."

The days and weeks wore on, and neither girl spoke about their encounter with the old woman. Both were busily preparing for the important day when their mother the queen would announce which princess would be her successor. Anita was almost certain it would be her. She was smart, a gifted leader, and was good with money. Anna, on the other hand, wasn't so sure. First, she didn't even know if she wanted to be queen. There were so many responsibilities. And she truly doubted whether or not she would be a good queen. She knew she could be disorganized and dreamy. What if she forgot some important event?

On the very day of the gala, the evening when the announcement of who the next queen would be, Anita was in her room, doing her hair and choosing her gown. While she was getting ready, there was a knock on her door. "Whoever could that be, she thought rather grumpily."

Well, at her door, was none other than the little old lady. She looked exactly as she had during her previous visit— black cloak, craggy face, and a big nose. Exasperated, Anita exclaimed, "What do *you* want. Can't you see I'm busy?"

The old lady didn't seem to care. "Excuse me," said the old crone, but do you have a minute for me to ask you another question?"

"Go ahead," Anita replied, "but make it quick."

"The last time I visited you, I asked whether or not you might share ½ of Snoitcarf with my people. Since you didn't think that was possible, what about a smaller portion, what about ¼ of Snoitcarf? My country is suffering. Please help us."

Anita couldn't believe this old woman was back. She immediately answered. "We don't have one-half of our country to share and we don't have one-fourth. Go somewhere else looking for charity. And please leave. I'm getting ready for a very important event."

And the old woman left with these words, "As you wish."

Well, on that same fateful day, Anna was dreamily sitting in the garden, looking at the hummingbirds and butterflies. As always, she was lost in her own world. She didn't even hear the little old lady approach. When the old crone tapped her on the shoulder, Anna jumped. "Oh, whatever do you want? You startled me!"

The old lady replied. "As you remember, the last time I visited you, I asked whether or not you might be able to share ½ of Snoitcarf with my people. Now I am asking if you could perhaps share even more. Would you be able to share ¾ of your beautiful country? My people are suffering. Please help us."

Anna took her time thinking about this dilemma. "Well," she mused, "Perhaps we could help. Our people are very kind and generous. They may be able to help your people get started…they could help them find jobs and help build homes. But I cannot make that decision on my own. I must ask my mother, the queen."

And the old woman left with these words, "As you wish."

That evening thousands of people were gathering at the great hall in the capital city of Snoitcarf. The girls were nervous, but excited. Anita wore a beautiful red dress with sequins. Anna wore a light blue dress that sparkled in the lights. On the main stage of the great hall sat three thrones. The middle one was the biggest and was reserved for the queen. The two thrones on either side were smaller and the two princesses were to sit there. As was always the ritual for large events, the twin princesses went out first to their thrones. As they walked out, the crowed cheered. The people of Snoitcarf were anxious to see who their new queen would be. The excitement in the air was palpable. And then the trumpets played the fanfare, which announced the queen's arrival. The crowd hushed. All awaited the queen.

But instead of the queen walking out onto the stage, out walked THE LITTLE OLD LADY! The crowd gasped. The girls looked at one another, eyes wide with amazement. Once the old lady made it to the center of the stage, she ripped the craggy mask off her face and threw off her black cloak. And under the mask and cape was none other than THE QUEEN! Both Anna and Anita couldn't believe their eyes. The queen looked at both girls and then at the crowd.

"I have made my decision. Both of my girls have excellent qualities. But I must choose the one who has the kindest heart, the one who will be generous and good to all people. I choose Anna to be your next queen."

The crowed cheered and clapped, for they knew that Anna was kind and good hearted and that she would always take their needs into consideration first. And the people of Snoitcarf lived happily ever after.

APPENDIX 2: BELLARMINE UNIVERSITY MASTER'S, RANK ONE, AND KENTAHTEN TEACHER TRAINING

The Bellarmine University Master of Arts Degree in education offers educators an opportunity to become more familiar with Waldorf education and its unique arts-based pedagogy. Waldorf-inspired teaching is designed to meet the needs of all learners, based on best practices in education. It features an integration of storytelling, music, movement, art, drama, and poetry into the teaching of academic subjects. The deeply integrated presentation of material has been shown to help engage children in the learning process and sustain their mastery of subject matter.

Kentahten Teacher Training is a developing Waldorf training for those wishing to teach in a private Waldorf school or for teachers desiring to use Waldorf-inspired methods in their public-school classrooms. This training is located at Bellarmine University in Louisville, Kentucky. The word *Kentahten* is a Native American term for Kentucky, meaning "Land of Tomorrow." Waldorf education is healing and beneficial for all learners. The education provided by Waldorf methods helps students realize their potential in the world, allowing them to make respectful, compassionate, responsible decisions that positively impact our global community. As we move forward in the twenty-first century and into the "tomorrow" that children will inherit, these are crucial qualities for our students to learn. Kentahten Teacher Training is committed to educating the whole child and nurturing the inner lives of teachers and administrators.

Waldorf Education aspires to:
- awaken imagination and wonder
- enliven and expand the breadth of student learning, bringing joy to the classroom
- address the developmental needs of all children, including those with special needs, through integrated, arts-filled learning

- enhance and enliven the multicultural aspect of history and language arts through stories, myths, folk tales and legends of various cultures
- use creativity in the classroom while nurturing emotional intelligence, kindness and responsibility through character building activities
- benefit students of a variety of backgrounds with an experiential and integrated approach
- strengthen literacy and numeracy with innovative and practical methods

Teachers learn to:
- protect childhood by creating a healthy and nurturing environment
- cultivate creative play activities
- energize a love of learning

The three-year program features eighteen credit hours of core courses and eighteen credit hours of courses with a Waldorf emphasis. The Waldorf-inspired courses are offered during a full-day, two-week institute each summer for three consecutive summers. Core courses are offered in the evening during the fall and spring semesters.

Waldorf-inspired courses are also available to individuals seeking a Kentucky Rank I certification and as a non-credit option through the School Continuing and Professional Studies or Kentahten Teacher Training.

For more information and current schedule, contact:

Dr. Mary Goral
Annsley Frazier Thornton School of Education
Bellarmine University / 2001 Newburg Road
Louisville, KY 40205
502.452.8146 / mgoral@bellarmine.edu

Summer I: Two-Week, All-Day Institute

Summer I	Master's	Rank One	Kentahten Training
Eurythmy/Singing/Intro to Waldorf Education 8:30–9:15	Optional	Suggested	Required
Child Development 9:30–12:30 (3 cr)	Required (core)	Suggested	Required
Weaving the Arts into the Sciences 1:30–4:30 (3 cr)	Required (elective)	Suggested	Required
Study Group: 6:00–8:00 p.m., T/Th, 12:30–1:30, W/F	Optional	Suggested	Required

Fall I: August–December, Wednesday and Thursday evenings

Fall I	Master's	Rank One	Kentahten Training
Advanced Curriculum 4:30–7:00, Wed. (3 cr)	Required (core)	Optional	Optional
Study Group 6:30–8:30 Thursdays, bimonthly	Optional	Optional	Required

Spring I: January–May, Wednesday and Thursday evenings

Spring I	Master's	Rank One	Kentahten Training
Diagnostic Reading 4:30–7:00, Wed. (3 cr)	Required (core)	Optional	Optional
Study Group 6:00–8:00 Thursdays, bimonthly	Optional	Optional	Required

Summer II: Two-Week, All-Day Institute

Summer II	Master's	Rank One	Kentahten Training
Eurythmy/Singing/Intro to Waldorf Education 8:30–9:15	Optional	Optional	Required
Teaching Mathematics in the Waldorf School 9:30–12:30 (3 cr)	Required (elective)	Suggested	Required
Art I: 1:30–4:30 (3 cr)	Required (elective)	Suggested	Required
Study Group: 6:00–8:00 p.m., T/Th, 12:30–1:30, W/F	Optional	Optional	Required

Fall II: August–December, Wednesday and Thursday evenings

Fall II	Master's	Rank One	Kentahten Training
Research 4:30–7:00 Wed. (3 cr)	Required (core)	Suggested	Optional
Study Group 6:30–8:30 Thursdays, bimonthly	Optional	Optional	Required

Spring II: January–May, Wednesday and Thursday evenings

Spring II	Master's	Rank One	Kentahten Training
Study Group 6:30–8:30 Thursdays, bimonthly	Suggested (elective)	Suggested	Required

Summer III: Two-Week, All-Day Institute

Summer III	Master's	Rank One	Kentahten Training
Eurythmy/Singing 8:30–9:15	Optional	Optional	Required
Sing me the Creation: Teaching Language Arts in the Waldorf School 9:30–12:30 (3 cr)	Required (elective)	Suggested	Required
Art II: 1:30–4:30 (3 cr)	Required (elective)	Suggested	Required
Study Group 6:00–8:00	Optional	Optional	Optional
Technology Course TBA (3 cr)	Required (core)	Optional	Optional

Fall III: August–December, Wednesday and Thursday evenings

Fall III	Master's	Rank One	Kentahten Training
Parent, Schools, Community 4:30–7:00 Wed. (3 cr)	Required (core)	Optional	Optional
Teaching Geography in the Waldorf School 6:00–8:00 Thurs. (2 cr)	Optional (elective)	Suggested	Required

Spring III: January–May, Thursday Evenings

Spring III	Master's	Rank One	Kentahten Training
Teaching History and Multicultural Education in the Waldorf School 6:00–8:00 (2 cr)	Optional (elective)	Suggested	Required

Summer IV: Ten-Day Course, Rudolf Steiner College, Sacramento, California

Summer IV	Master's	Rank One	Kentahten Training
Capstone Anthroposophic Study Courses, Art	Optional	Optional	Required

- Master's candidates will complete thirty-six credit hours. Eighteen hours will be in courses with a Waldorf emphasis and eighteen hours will be in traditional education courses. Receiving a master's degree from Bellarmine will not result in state teaching certification.

- Kentucky Rank One Students need to choose thirty hours to receive their Rank One status. A Rank One is for those teachers who already have a master's degree in education.

- The thirty credit hours above the master's can be made up in a variety of ways. The Waldorf-inspired courses are offered for those people interested in learning more about Waldorf education.

- Kentahten Teacher Training Students will complete eighteen credit hours during summers, eight credit hours in fall and spring. Students seeking Waldorf Training will also complete two field experiences. During Spring I (or Summer II), students will complete an early field experience that consists of observation and assisting in a Waldorf classroom. During Spring II (or Summer

III), students will complete a practicum where they will teach a block or part of a block in a Waldorf school. During Summer IV, students will complete a ten-day Capstone experience at the Rudolf Steiner College.

- Bellarmine University will not offer the certification in Waldorf education. Our training program will be under the auspices of AWSNA (Association of Waldorf Schools of North America).
- Financial Aid is available for those wishing to complete the master's degree.
- Limited/partial scholarships are available for master's work, Rank One, and Kentahten Training.

BIBLIOGRAPHY

Armstrong, T. (1994). *Multiple Intelligences in the Classroom*. Alexandria, VA: ASCD.

———. (2006). *The Best Schools: How Human Development Research Should Inform Educational Practice*. Alexandria, VA: ASCD.

Arrien, A. (2001). The way of the teacher: Principals of deep engagement. Linda Lantieri (Ed.), *Schools with Spirit: Nurturing the Inner Lives of Children and Teachers*. Boston, MA: Beacon Press.

Association of Waldorf Schools of North America. (1992). Membership directory. [Brochure]. Fair Oaks, CA: Author.

Ayers, B. (1995). *To Become a Teacher: Making a Difference in Children's Lives*. NY: Teachers College Press.

———. (2004). *Teaching toward Freedom: Moral Commitment and Ethical Action in the Classroom*. Boston, MA: Beacon Press.

Barnes, H. (1980). An introduction to Waldorf education. *Teachers College Record*, 81 (Spring), 323-336.

———. (1999). Helping children to develop respect and wonder. *Renewal*, 8 (2), 5-7.

Biddulph, S. (1998). *Raising Boys: Why Boys Are Different and How to Help Them Become Happy and Well-Balanced Men*. Berkley, CA: Celestial Arts.

Byers, P., Dillard, C., Easton, F., Manry, M., McDermott, R., Oberman, I., and Urmacher, B. (1996). *Waldorf education in an inner city public school: The Urban Waldorf School of Milwaukee*. Spring Valley, NY: Parker Courtney Press.

Comer, J., Haynes, N., Joyner, E., and Ben-Avie, M. (Eds.) (1996). *Rallying the Whole Village: The Comer Process for Reforming Education*. New York: Teachers College Press.

———. (1998). Rallying the whole village. *Encounter*, 11(4), 4-12.

Conte, Z. (2001). The gift of the arts. Linda Lantieri (Ed.), *Schools with Spirit: Nurturing The Inner Lives of Children and Teachers.* Boston, MA: Beacon Press.

Dewey, J. (1910). *How to Think.* Boston, MA: Heath.

Edmunds, F. (1992). *Rudolf Steiner Education: The Waldorf School.* Sussex, England: Rudolf Steiner College Press.

Eisner, E. (1994). *Cognition and Curriculum Reconsidered.* New York: Teachers College Press.

———. (2002). *The Arts and the Creation of the Mind.* London: Yale University Press.

Emmons, C., Comer, J., and Haynes, N. (1996). Translating theory into practice: Comer's theory of school reform. Comer, J., Haynes, N., Joyner, E., and Ben-Avie, M. (Eds.). *Rallying the Whole Village: The Comer Process for Reforming Education.* New York: Teachers College Press.

Fowler, C. (1996). *Strong Arts, Strong Schools: The Promising Potential and Shortsighted Disregard of the Arts in American Schools.* New York: Oxford University Press.

Fox, M. (2006). *The A. W. E. Project: Reinventing Education, Reinventing the Human.* BC Canada: CopperHouse Books.

Froebel, F. (1887). *The Education of Man.* Translated and annotated by W. N. Hailmann. New York: Appleton.

Galeano, E. (2004). Celebration of the human voice. Paul Loeb (Ed.), *The Impossible Will Take a Little While: A Citizen's Guide to Hope in a Time of Fear.* New York: Basic Books.

Gardner, H. (1983). *Frames of Mind: The Theory of Multiple Intelligences.* New York: Basic Books.

———. (1993). *Multiple Intelligences: The Theory in Practice.* New York: Basic Books.

Goodman, J. (1992). *Elementary Schooling for Critical Democracy.* Albany, NY: State University of New York Press.

Goral, M. (2000). A connective pedagogy. *Paths of Learning,* 2 (6), 54-60.

——— and Gnadinger, C. (2006). Using storytelling to teach mathematics concepts. *Australian Primary Mathematics Classroom,* 11(1), 4-8.

Grant, J., Johnson, B., and Richardson, J. (1996). *The Looping Handbook: Teachers and Students Progressing Together.* Petersborough, NH: Crystal Springs.

Gutek, G. (1968). *Pestalozzi and Education.* New York: Longman.

Havel, V. (2004). An orientation of the heart. Paul Loeb (Ed.), *The Impossible Will Take a Little While: A Citizen's Guide to Hope in a Time of Fear.* New York: Basic Books.

Hooks, b. (1999). Embracing freedom: Spirituality and liberation. Steven Glazer (Ed.), *The Heart of Learning.* New York: Tarcher/Putnam.

Intrator, S. (Ed.) (2002). *Stories of the Courage to Teach: Honoring the Teacher's Heart.* San Francisco, CA: Jossey-Bass.

———— and Kunzman, R. (2006). Starting with the soul. *Educational Leadership,* 63(6), 38-43.

Jamison, R. (1995). Waldorf methods applied in the public school. [Brochure].

Jensen, E. (1998). *Teaching with the Brain in Mind.* Alexandria, VA: ASCD.

————. (2000?). *Arts with the Brain in Mind.* Alexandria, VA: ASCD.

Jung, C. (1973). *Answer to Job* (R.F.C. Hull, Trans.), Princeton, NJ: Princeton University Press.

Kessler, R. (2000). *The Soul of Education: Helping Students Find Connection, Compassion and Character at School.* Alexandria, VA: ASCD.

Koetzsch, R. (1989). Waldorf Schools: Education for the Head, Hands, and Heart. *Utne Reader* (May).

Korten, D. (2006). *The Great Turning: From Empire to Earth Community.* San Francisco, CA: Berrett-Koehler Publishers.

Louv, R. (2005). *Last Child in the Woods: Saving Our Children from Nature Deficit Disorder.* Chapel Hill, NC: Algonquin Books.

Miller, R. (1999). Holistic education for an emerging culture. Steven Glazer (Ed.), *The Heart of Learning.* New York: Tarcher/Putnam.

Moore, P. (1996). Hearts for the homeless. *Arts and Activities.* 120(4), 36.

Noddings, N. (1992). *The Challenge to Care in Schools: An Alternative Approach to Education.* New York: Teachers College Press.

————. (2005). What does it mean to educate the whole child? *Educational Leadership,* 63(1), 8-13.

Ogletree, E. (1970). Teaching number sense through rhythmical counting. *Elementary School Journal,* 71(1), 11-17.

————. (1974). Rudolf Steiner: Unknown educator. *The Elementary School Journal,* 74 (March), 345-351.

Orr, D. (1999). Reassembling the pieces: Architecture as pedagogy. Steven Glazer (Ed.), *The Heart of Learning.* New York: Tarcher/Putnam.

Palmer, P. (1999). The grace of great things: Reclaiming the sacred in knowing, teaching and learning. Steven Glazer (Ed.), *The Heart of Learning.* New York: Tarcher/Putnam.

————. (2002). What I heard them say. Sam Intrator (Ed.), *Stories of the Courage to Teach: Honoring the Teacher's Heart*. San Francisco, CA: Jossey-Bass.

Petrash, J. (2002). *Understanding Waldorf Education: Teaching from the Inside Out*. Beltsville, MD: Gryphon House.

Rawson, M. & Richter, T. (eds.) (2000). *The Educational Tasks and Content of the Steiner Waldorf Curriculum*. East Sussex, UK: Steiner Schools Fellowship Publications.

Reinsmith, W. (1989). The whole in every part: Steiner and Waldorf schooling. *Educational Forum, 54* (Fall), 79-92.

Remen, R.N. (1999). Educating for mission, meaning, and compassion. Steven Glazer (Ed.), *The Heart of Learning*. New York: Tarcher/Putnam.

Richards, M.C. (1980). *Towards Wholeness: Rudolf Steiner Education in America*. Middleton, CT: Wesleyan University Press.

Robinson, S. and Darling-Hammond, L. (2005). Change for collaboration and collaboration for change: Transforming teaching through school-university change. Linda Darling-Hammond (Ed.), *Professional Development Schools: Schools for Developing a Profession*. New York: Teachers College Press.

Rockne, J. (2002). Teaching had become an ordinary job. Sam Intrator (Ed.), *Stories of the Courage to Teach: Honoring the Teacher's Heart*. San Francisco, CA: Jossey-Bass.

Roddick, A. (1998). Social responsibility in business. Eddie and Debbie Shapiro (Ed.), *Voices from the Heart: Inspirations for a Compassionate Future*. NY: Tarcher/Putnam.

Stafford, V. (2004). The small work in the great work. Paul Loeb (Ed.), *The Impossible Will Take a Little While: A Citizen's Guide to Hope in a Time of Fear*. New York: Basic Books.

Staley, B. (1997). The Waldorf approach within public education. *Illinois Schools Journal, 77*(1), 15-31.

Steiner, R. (1996). *The Child's Changing Consciousness as the Basis of Pedagogical Practice*. Hudson, NY: Anthroposophic Press.

————. (1997). *The Roots of Education*. Hudson, NY: Anthroposophic Press.

————. (2000). *Practical Advice to Teachers*. Great Barrington, MA: Anthroposophic Press.

————. (2003). *Soul Economy: Body, Soul, and Spirit in Waldorf Education*. Great Barrington, MA: Anthroposophic Press.

————. (2004). *The Spiritual Ground of Education*. Great Barrington, MA: Anthroposophic Press.

————. (2007). *Balance in Teaching*. Great Barrington, MA: Anthroposophic Press.

Sturbaum, M. (1997). *Transformational Possibilities of Schooling: A Study of Waldorf Education*. Unpublished doctoral dissertation. Indiana University, Bloomington.

Williams, L., Oberman, I. & Goral, M. (2008). Proposal to AERA. Unpublished raw data.

Wolf, A. (1996). *Nurturing the Spirit in Non-Sectarian Classrooms*. Hollidaysburg, PA: Parent Child Press.

Wolk, S. (2007). Why go to school? *Phi Delta Kappan*. 88 (9): 648-658.

Wood, F., Thompson, S., and Russell, S.F. (1981). Designing effective staff development programs. Betty Dillon-Peterson (Ed.), *Staff Development/Organization Development*. Alexandria, VA: ASCD.

Wood, G. (1992). *Schools that Work: American's Most Innovative Public Education Programs*. New York: Penguin.

Urmacher, B. (1991). *Waldorf Schools Marching along Quietly Unheard*. Unpublished doctoral dissertation, Stanford University.

————. (1994). Interview with Elliott Eisner. Unpublished raw data.

Zemelman, S., Daniels, H., and Hyde, A. (1998). *Best Practice: New Standards for Teaching and Learning in America's Schools*. Portsmouth, NH: Heinemann.